More MICROWAVE BOTTLING

Isabel Webb

The Five Mile Press

The Five Mile Press

The Five Mile Press Pty. Ltd.
67 Rushdale Street
Knoxfield Victoria 3180 Australia

First published under the title
Low Sugar Microwave Bottling in 1990

This new edition first published 1994

Copyright © text Isabel Webb
Design and illustrations by Geoff Hocking
Photography by Mannix

All rights reserved. No part of this publication may be reproduced, stored in, or introduced into a retrieval system, or transmitted in any form by any means whatsoever without the prior permission of the Publishers.

Every precaution has been taken to ensure the safety of the microwave bottling method. If the directions are not followed accurately, the author and publisher cannot accept responsibility for damage to persons or property.

Typeset by Post Typesetters, Brisbane, Qld
Printed in Singapore by Kyodo Printing Co. Ltd.

National Library of Australia Cataloguing-in-Publication Data

Webb, Isabel, 1936-
More microwave bottling.

ISBN 0 86788 881 4

1. Food — Preservation. 2. Fruit — Preservation.
3. Microwave cookery. I. Title.

641.42

CONTENTS

Preface
Page 1

Before You Begin
Page 3

1
'Just Fruit' Bottling
Page 6

2
Low-sugar Whole Fruit Jams
Page 30

3
Savoury Sauces
Page 43

4
Chutneys, Relishes and Pickles
Page 53

5
Fruit and Nut Butters
Page 65

6
Sugarless Fruit Spreads
Page 71

7
Fruit Drinks and Cordials
Page 77

8
Fruits Roli-ups
Page 85

Conversion Table
Page 88

Index
Page 89

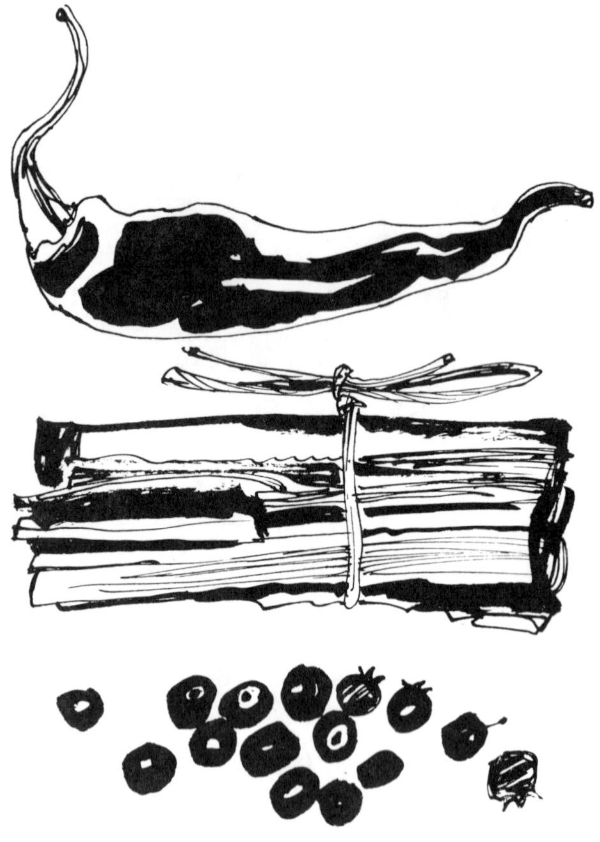

Preface

Food preserving is coming back into its own, not only because of the convenience of modern methods, but for the perennial reasons of quality, economy, and variety in the winter months. And the recycling of used commercial food jars for home bottling makes sense both economically and from the environmental viewpoint.

But who would have thought we'd ever see the day when fruit preserving was possible without sugar or water? I didn't, until the microwave oven came along — and then it seemed possible.

I knew that many people would benefit enormously if a sugarless or low-sugar bottling method could be developed, and I felt sure it could be done. So it was back to the drawing board — or kitchen bench — to experiment.

The results, published in this book, will astound you. With much of the jar no longer filled with syrups or water, more space is available for all those natural juices, and the end result is full of flavour and nourishment. Furthermore, the process is faster than any other used to date.

My first book, *Microwave Bottling,* introduced the microwave method of preserving fruit, jellies, jams, pickles and sauces. This book now shows you how to preserve all of these *with minimal — or, in some cases, no — added sugar.*

The recipes in this book therefore add a nutritional bonus to the convenience of microwave fruit preserving and are particularly suited to the health- and weight-conscious.

I wish you success in your adventures into the world of low- or no-sugar microwave bottling.

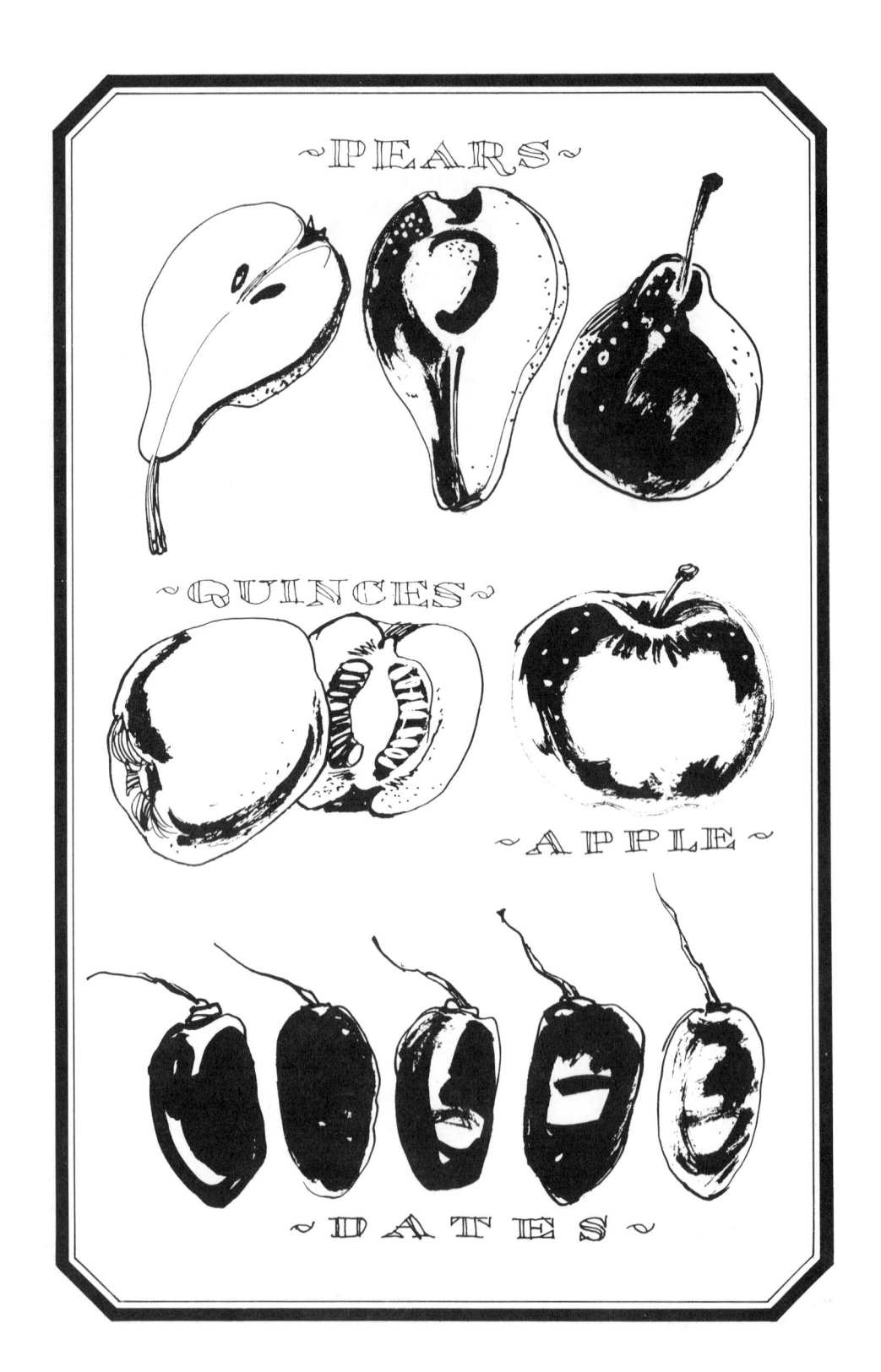

~PEARS~

~QUINCES~

~APPLE~

~DATES~

Before You Begin

General

- Make sure the jars to be used fit in your microwave oven with their lids on.
- Make sure there's no excess water on the microwave carousel.
- Always cover the bowl for the first cooking in the microwave. Once sugar or sweetener is added, cook without the cover so moisture can come away.

Power variations

Remember that every microwave oven is slightly different, and power supplies can vary, especially at peak times or when several appliances are being run from the same circuit. The cooking times will prove more accurate if you clean and dry the microwave carousel before you start. Any moisture will use up microwave energy and could affect cooking time.

Setting

HIGH	= 100 per cent microwaves
MEDIUM–HIGH	= 75 per cent microwaves
MEDIUM	= 50 per cent microwaves

Metal

There's no need to worry about placing a small amount of metal in your microwave oven. The small ratio of metal compound to other substances involved in the bottling process will not cause any arcing or damage to the oven. As a precaution, always allow a space of at least 3 cm (1¼ in) between jars and the oven wall.

Shelf life

All recipes in this book can be kept for a long period, but for optimum colour and flavour it is wise to use them within 12 months. Then they can be replaced with new season's fruit.

Never...

...preserve vegetables in your microwave. Government health authorities warn that this could be fatal.

Equipment

The microwave method eliminates the need for elaborate equipment. You will need:
- a large microwave-proof bowl with a cover
- a spoon, preferably wooden
- jars or bottles.

Jars or bottles of various shapes and sizes can be used, providing they are fitted with a rubber ring and a metal lid, plus a device that holds the lid firmly in position, such as a metal screw band, a clip or a metal spring cap. Make sure the jars fit in your oven with their lids on.

Recycled jars

Recycled jars (for instance, those used for commercial jam and marmalade) are ideal for microwave bottling, provided:
- Their lids are the metal screw-on variety, in good condition. Metal lids are treated on the inside with a special food lacquer to protect them from corrosive food acids. It is important to check that this film is not damaged in any way and that the lids are in 'as new' condition and fit perfectly. Please note that plastic lids must *not* be used.

- The lids are fitted with a built-in rubber sealing ring.
- The jars are not chipped or cracked. Their rims must be smooth and free from any chips, ridges or any imperfections. Damaged jars won't seal properly and the fruit will spoil.

Preserving jars

If you use conventional preserving jars, fit new rubber rings for each bottling. Check the clips, too, as older clips tend to lose their spring and may not hold the lids firmly in place during the sealing process.

Sterilising your equipment

1. Clean jars thoroughly in hot water, removing any adhesions with a bottle brush before sterilising.

2. Half-fill jars with cold water and cook on HIGH until water boils (approximately 2 minutes per jar).

3. Remove jars from microwave and fill the lids of the jars with the hot water. If rubber gaskets are to be used, drop each gasket into its jar of hot water and leave for a few minutes.

4. Pour away water before fruit is packed into jars.

1

'JUST FRUIT' BOTTLING

This type of bottling involves just fruit — nothing else — hence the name of this chapter. You can use this method to preserve a single piece of fruit, a full jar or even half a jar.

Because fruit has such a high water content, it can be preserved in the microwave with no additives, *not even water*. The microwave acts very quickly on the fruit juices to create the temperature required to preserve (83°C/180°F). Excess air will be expelled on heating, so partly filled jars do not present a problem. During cooking a little fruit juice may appear, but the fruit will hold its shape.

Once sealed in the jar, fruit has a high nutritional value, good keeping qualities, and outstanding colour, texture and flavour.

'Just fruit' is ideal for a single serve, a special diet or simply a change. On serving, the fruit can be sweetened to taste with artificial sweeteners, sugar, honey or golden syrup.

'Just fruit', served with a topping or ice-cream, makes a mouth-watering, nourishing dessert for children.

Some general points

- Fruit and microwave ovens go hand in hand. Fruit has a high moisture content, which is converted to heat energy by the microwaves. During the preserving process itself, 83°C (180°F) is sufficiently high a temperature to destroy bacteria,

expel any excess air from the jars and cause an optimum vacuum.
- Bottling fruit without adding liquid shortens the cooking time, as only the fruit has to heat to the required temperature. This occurs very quickly once the microwave is turned on.
- A processed bottle of fruit seals approximately 5 minutes after leaving the microwave oven, as cooling takes place.
- Metal lids must be used, as metal has a higher coefficient of expansion than glass, and any expanding air and liquid has space to escape between lid and jar.

Alternative sweeteners

With the 'just fruit' method of bottling, sweeteners may be added to the fruit in the jar before preserving, or the fruit may be sweetened to taste on serving. If added before preserving, the sweetener might not dissolve immediately, but it will do so after standing for a while. The following quantities are suggested:

Granulated sugar:	1 dessertspoon per cup of fruit
Honey or golden syrup:	1 tablespoon per cup of fruit
Artificial sweeteners:	Add to taste. These are best added on serving, because cooking and storage can cause bitterness. Once opened, any left-over fruit that has been artificially sweetened must be kept refrigerated.

Liquids

As already mentioned, liquid need not be added with this method of preserving, as natural fruit juices are expelled on cooking. However, if more juice is required, cover the base of the jar with 1 cm (½ in) of cold water before adding the fruit.

Cooking times

The cooking times in this book are for one jar in a 650-watt microwave oven. If you wish to preserve more than one jar, or your microwave is not 650 watt, please note the following adjustments, which apply to jars of any size:

- For each additional jar in a *650-watt capacity* oven add 1 minute cooking time, unless otherwise specified.
- *500–550-watt capacity:* Allow 1 extra minute of cooking time per jar.
- *700-watt capacity:* Deduct 30 seconds' cooking time for every jar.
- *750-watt capacity:* Same cooking time as for 650-watt, but microwave setting on MEDIUM (50%).

With the 'just fruit' method of bottling, jars may be only partly full. But remember that if you have only one cup of fruit in a two-cup jar, you must calculate your cooking time by the amount of fruit, not by the jar size.

Don't use more than 4 jars at any one time, as the cooking times will alter.

Cup measurements

In the following recipes the amount of fruit is sometimes given in cupfuls. Please note that these are approximate measures only, as fruit sizes vary.

Preparing and packing the fruit

1 Never use fruit straight from the refrigerator. Always use it at room temperature.

2 Choose unblemished fruit. Wash well in cold water.

3 Peel, core, slice or dice fruit according to recipe. Check recipe for any pre-cooking, soaking or other preparation necessary.

4 Pack fruit into clean, warm, sterilised jars. If filling jars to capacity, leave 1 cm (½ in) below the lip of the jar. Gently tap the bottom of each jar on the palm of your hand to ensure firm packing. But don't worry if jars are not filled to capacity, as air will be expelled during cooking. (The metal lid will expand on heating, allowing excess air to escape.)

5 If using clip-top jars, fit rubber gaskets in position and clip down lids. If using screw-top jars, screw lids on lightly. Tighten lids as soon as jars are removed from oven.

Citric acid

Some fruits (for example cantaloupe and mangoes) are low in natural fruit acids and will not preserve successfully unless citric acid is added. Check individual recipes for amounts required.

Apricots, apples, peaches and pears

To help prevent the discolouration of these fruits during storage, soak prepared fruit in a solution of 2 cups water to the juice of one lemon for a few minutes before rinsing and cooking. (Or you could instead add 2 strips of lemon rind and bottle these with the fruit.) A little water (no more than ⅓ of the jar) may be added before preserving these fruits. This helps prevent the fruit acids browning the exposed fruit at the top of the jar.

Cooking the fruit

Each recipe contains a table showing oven settings and cooking times required to bring the inside of the fruit to 83°C (180°F), thus eliminating all microbes and ensuring a good seal. The times given are those needed for firm, ripe fruit at room temperature. Less cooking time is needed for soft fruits such as grapes and berries than for hard fruits such as apples and pears, as you will see from individual recipes.

Arrange jars in a circle on the carousel, leaving at least 3 cm (1¼ in) between each jar and oven wall.

Cooling the fruit and checking the seal

1 After cooking, remove jars from microwave oven and stand on a rack, a board or several sheets of newspaper to cool.

2 If using clip-top jars, gently press down lids without removing the clip. If using screw-top jars, screw lids down tightly. Use a cloth to avoid burning your hands on the hot lids.

3 Allow jars to cool for several hours or overnight before removing the spring clips.

4 Stand cold jars upside-down for at least 1 hour and check for any leakage. If leakage occurs, the jars have not sealed.

5 If jars have not sealed, immediately replace rubber gaskets and re-process in microwave for same time as previously. Then repeat steps 1-4. If fruit is not re-processed, it must be refrigerated and eaten within 2-3 days.

6 If there is no leakage and lids remain firm, a good vacuum has been achieved and the fruit will keep well.

Storing the fruit

1 Label and date jars.

2 Store in a cool, dark place.

3 All the preserved food in this book can be kept for long periods, but for optimum colour, flavour and nutritional value use within 12 months.

4 Once opened, jars of preserved fruit must be stored in the refrigerator and eaten within 2-3 days.

*Do*s and *don't*s

The following is a checklist of the main *do*s and *don't*s of microwave fruit bottling:

- Make sure fruit is of good, sound quality and is at room temperature.
- Clean fruit well in cold water before placing in sterilised jars. Soak apricots, apples, peaches and

pears as described on page 10 to prevent discolouration.
- Don't worry if jars are not quite dry, as a little moisture helps the fruit slide into position.
- Don't use rusty, damaged or pitted lids.
- If using screw-on lids, screw down tightly after cooking.
- Don't let the rubber gasket become twisted. A little water will help you to flick the gasket into its correct position.
- Make sure lids and clips are firmly secured.
- Check that your oven is on the correct setting — MEDIUM–HIGH.
- After cooking, stand jars on a cake rack, chopping board or several thicknesses of newspaper. This prevents damage to jars and surfaces.
- Don't remove clips while bottles are still hot. Allow to cool overnight or for several hours.
- Check the seal (see pages 10-11). If no liquid oozes out you have achieved a good result. If liquid escapes, the rubber gasket may need replacing, fruit may be caught under the screw-on type lid or the wrong lid may have been used. Rectify the problem before reprocessing in the oven. Alternatively, the fruit must be treated as any other jar of fruit just opened, and eaten within a couple of days.
- Store in a cool, dark place to ensure good colour and nutritional value for an optimum period.
- Don't use a bottle opener to remove lids. Always turn jar upside-down and break seal with a pointed knife by placing it between lid and rubber gasket and pressing down firmly.
- Don't try to reseal a half-used jar. Once a jar has been opened, the contents must be kept refrigerated and used within a few days.

Common pitfalls

Below are some common microwave bottling problems and the most likely reasons for them:

PROBLEM	MOST LIKELY REASON
Fruit of poor colour	• Over-ripe fruit used • Jar processed for too long • Storage area either too light or too warm
Jar didn't seal	• Rubber gasket perished • Rubber gasket twisted • Fruit lodged between gasket and rim of jar • Bruised, damaged or over-ripe fruit used • Bottled fruit not cooked long enough, so perfect seal not achieved • Jar not stored in cool, dark place. Mould and fermentation have affected seal. • Bacteria formed. This sometimes occurs in low-acid fruits. Check the recipe for the correct quantity of citric acid to be added. • An unclean, unsterilised jar was used.
Apricots, apples, peaches or pears discoloured during storage	• Fruit acids have caused browning. Follow directions on page 10.

APPLES

(Circles, dice or quarters)

METHOD

1
Choose firm, ripe, unblemished apples. Peel and core, then dice, slice or quarter. Immerse in lemon water to prevent discolouration (See page 10).

2
Place in clean, sterilised jars. Add sweetener if desired.

3
Fit lids according to instructions on page 9.

4
Cook as follows:

FRUIT	JAR SIZE	OVEN SETTING	COOKING TIME
1 apple	200–300 ml	medium–high	2 mins
2 apples	350–450 ml	medium–high	3 mins
3 apples	550–650 ml	medium–high	5 mins

(Note: For every additional jar add 1 minute's cooking time.)

5
Cool and store as directed on pages 10–11.

~ APPLE ~

APPLE PUREE FOR PIES

INGREDIENTS
Cooking apples, 6–8
Water, 125ml (½ cup)
Optional: Sugar, 250g (1 cup)

METHOD

1
Wash apples and chop roughly. There is no need to peel or core them.

2
Place chopped fruit and water in a microwave-proof bowl. Cook on HIGH until soft and pulpy (approximately 10 minutes).

3
Remove from oven and allow to stand, covered, for 5 minutes.

4
Press mixture through a sieve or Mouli, to puree. Stir in sugar (if using).

5
Fill clean, warm, sterilised jars to brim with apple pulp.

6
Fit lids according to instructions on page 9.

7
Cook as follows:

JAR SIZE	OVEN SETTING	COOKING TIME
250–350 ml	medium-high	2 mins
400–650 ml	medium-high	3 mins
800–900 ml	medium-high	4 mins

(Note: For every additional jar add 1 minute's cooking time.)

8
Cool and store as directed on pages 10–11.

APRICOTS

(Whole or halves)

METHOD

1
Choose firm, ripe, unblemished apricots. Use whole, or halve by cutting around the natural line with a stainless steel knife. Twist halves apart and remove and discard stones. Immerse in lemon water to prevent discolouration (see page 10).

2
Place in clean, sterilised jars with cut side facing down, and overlapping. Add sweetener if desired.

3
Fit lids according to instructions on page 9.

4
Cook as follows:

FRUIT	JAR SIZE	OVEN SETTING	COOKING TIME
4-5 apricots	200-300 ml	medium-high	2 mins
8-12 apricots	350-450 ml	medium-high	3 mins
20-25 apricots	550-650 ml	medium-high	5 mins

(Note: For every additional jar add 1 minute's cooking time.)

5
Cool and store as directed on pages 10-11.

~ APRICOTS ~

BERRIES

This method is suitable for most berries, including strawberries, raspberries, loganberries and blackberries.

METHOD

1
Choose full, ripe berries, making sure they are unblemished. Wash, and remove any stems.

2
Place berries in a microwave-proof bowl. Add sweetener if desired.

3
Cook on HIGH for 1 minute. Remove from oven and allow to stand until cool.

4
Place in clean, warm, sterilised jars.

5
Fit lids according to instructions on page 9.

6
Cook as follows:

FRUIT	JAR SIZE	OVEN SETTING	COOKING TIME
1 cup berries	200–300 ml	medium–high	1 mins
2 cups berries	350–450 ml	medium–high	2 mins
3 cups berries	550–650 ml	medium–high	4 mins

(Note: For every additional jar add 1 minute's cooking time.)

7
Cool and store as directed on pages 10–11.

CANTALOUPE (ROCKMELON)

(Balls or dice)

METHOD

1
Choose a firm, ripe cantaloupe.

2
Peel and seed fruit. With a baller, scoop out small balls, or slice or dice.

3
Place in clean sterilised jars. Add sweetener if desired.

4
For each cup of fruit add ½ teaspoon citric acid.

5
Fit lids according to instructions on page 9.

6
Cook as follows:

FRUIT	JAR SIZE	OVEN SETTING	COOKING TIME
1 cup cantaloupe	200–300 ml	medium–high	2 mins
2 cups cantaloupe	350–450 ml	medium–high	3 mins
3 cups cantaloupe	550–650 ml	medium–high	5 mins

(Note: For every additional jar add 1 minute's cooking time.)

6
Cool and store as directed on pages 10–11.

CHERRIES

METHOD

1
Choose ripe, unblemished cherries and wash well. Stone fruit with cherry stoner if desired.

2
Place fruit in clean, sterilised jars. Add sweetener if desired.

3
Fit lids according to instructions on page 9.

4
Cook as follows:

FRUIT	JAR SIZE	OVEN SETTING	COOKING TIME
1 cup cherries	200–300 ml	medium–high	2 mins
2 cups cherries	350–450 ml	medium–high	3 mins
3 cups cherries	550–650 ml	medium–high	5 mins

(Note: For every additional jar add 1 minute's cooking time.)

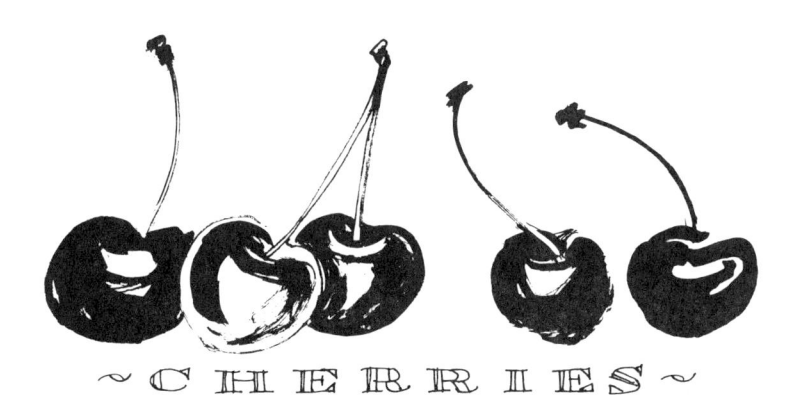

5
Cool and store as directed on pages 10–11.

~CHERRIES~

CHERRY PLUMS

METHOD

1
Choose ripe, unblemished cherry plums and wash well.

2
Place fruit in clean, sterilised jars. Add sweetener if desired.

3
Fit lids according to instructions on page 9.

4
Cook as follows:

FRUIT	JAR SIZE	OVEN SETTING	COOKING TIME
1 cup cherry plums	200–300 ml	medium–high	2 mins
2 cups cherry plums	350–450 ml	medium–high	3 mins
3 cups cherry plums	550–650 ml	medium–high	5 mins

(Note: For every additional jar add 1 minute's cooking time.)

5
Cool and store as directed on pages 10–11.

CITRUS FRUIT

(Grapefruit, oranges, mandarins)

METHOD

1
Choose unblemished fruit.

2
Peel, taking away all the pith, and remove segments by cutting down to centre of the fruit on each side of the segment's dividing line. Slip the knife in at the bottom of each segment and push it free. Set aside, ready for bottling.

3
Place in clean, sterilised jars. Add sweetener if desired.

4
Fit lids according to instructions on page 9.

5
Cook as follows:

FRUIT	JAR SIZE	OVEN SETTING	COOKING TIME
1 cup fruit	200–300 ml	medium–high	2 mins
2 cups fruit	350–450 ml	medium–high	3 mins
3 cups fruit	550–650 ml	medium–high	4 mins

(Note: For every additional jar add 1 minute's cooking time.)

6
Cool and store as directed on pages 10–11.

FRUIT SALAD

METHOD

1
Selection of fruits is important. Fruits low in natural acids are not recommended, e.g. bananas, cantaloupe, pawpaw, figs and mangoes, but these can be preserved separately (with citric acid) and added before serving. The most common fruits used are: apples, apricots, cherries, grapes, pineapple, peaches and oranges.

2
Peel if necessary. Cut or dice as desired.

3
Mix all fruits together. Add sweetener if desired.

4
Place in clean, sterilised jars.

5
Fit lids according to instructions on page 9.

6
Cook as follows:

FRUIT	JAR SIZE	OVEN SETTING	COOKING TIME
1 cup fruit	200–300 ml	medium-high	2 mins
2 cups fruit	350–450 ml	medium-high	3 mins
3 cups fruit	550–650 ml	medium-high	5 mins

(Note: For every additional jar add 1 minute's cooking time.)

7
Cool and store as directed on pages 10–11.

MANGOES

METHOD

1
Skin mangoes by peeling down from stem. The skin will come away easily if the fruit is ripe.

2
Cut flesh from seed and slice into wedges or pieces.

3
Place in clean, sterilised jars. Add sweetener if desired.

4
To each cup of fruit, add ½ teaspoon of citric acid.

5
Fit lids according to instructions on page 9.

6
Cook as follows:

FRUIT	JAR SIZE	OVEN SETTING	COOKING TIME
1 mango	200–300 ml	medium-high	2 mins
2 mangoes	350–450 ml	medium-high	3 mins
3 mangoes	550–650 ml	medium-high	4 mins

(Note: For every additional jar add 1 minute's cooking time.)

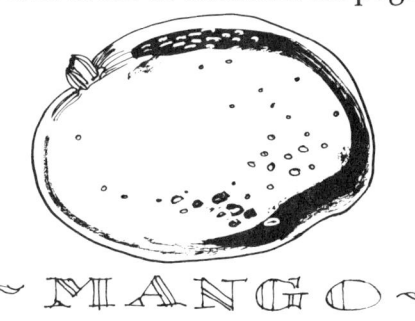

7
Cool and store as directed on pages 10-11.

~ MANGO ~

PEACHES

(Clingstone and freestone)

METHOD

1

Choose firm, ripe, unblemished peaches. Use whole, or halve by cutting around the natural line with a stainless steel knife. Twist halves apart and remove and discard stones. Remove peel. Immerse in lemon water to prevent discolouration (See page 10).

2

Place in clean, sterilised jars with cut side facing down, and overlapping. Add sweetener if desired.

3

Fit lids according to instructions on page 9.

4

Cook as follows:

FRUIT	JAR SIZE	OVEN SETTING	COOKING TIME
1 peach	200-300 ml	medium-high	2 mins
2 peaches	350-450 ml	medium-high	3 mins
3 peaches	550-650 ml	medium-high	5 mins

(Note: For every additional jar add 1 minute's cooking time.)

5

Cool and store as directed on pages 10-11.

~PEACHES~

PEARS

METHOD

1
Choose firm, ripe, unblemished pears. Peel, cut in half and scoop out core with a teaspoon. Immerse in lemon water to prevent discolouration (see page 10).

2
Place in clean, sterilised jars with cut side facing down. Add sweetener if desired.

3
Fit lids according to instructions on page 9.

4
Cook as follows:

FRUIT	JAR SIZE	OVEN SETTING	COOKING TIME
1 pear	200–300 ml	medium–high	2 mins
2 pears	350–450 ml	medium–high	3 mins
3 pears	550–650 ml	medium–high	4 mins

(Note: For every additional jar add 1 minute's cooking time.)

6
Cool and store as directed on pages 10–11.

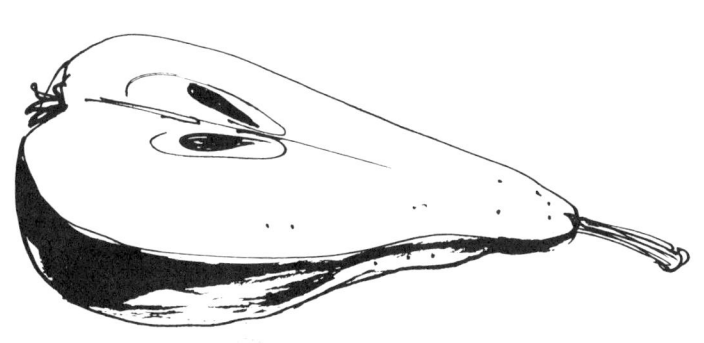

~ PEAR ~

Pineapple

(Wedges, circles or dice)

METHOD

1
Peel, eye and core pineapple.

2
Cut into wedges, circles or dice.

3
Place in clean, sterilised jars. Add sweetener if desired.

4
Fit lids according to instructions on page 9.

5
Cook as follows:

FRUIT	JAR SIZE	OVEN SETTING	COOKING TIME
1 cup pineapple	200–300 ml	medium-high	2 mins
2 cups pineapple	350–450 ml	medium-high	3 mins
3 cups pineapple	560–650 ml	medium-high	5 mins

(Note: For every additional jar add 1 minute's cooking time.)

6
Cool and store as directed on pages 10–11.

~ PINEAPPLE ~

Plums

METHOD

1
Choose firm, ripe, unblemished plums and wash well. Use whole, or halve by cutting around the natural line with a stainless steel knife. Twist halves apart and remove and discard stones.

2
If preserving whole, prick plums all over with a darning needle or skewer to prevent the skins from splitting while cooking.

3
Place in clean, sterilised jars, with cut side facing down and overlapping if halved. Add sweetener if desired.

4
Fit lids according to instructions on page 9.

5
Cook as follows:

FRUIT	JAR SIZE	OVEN SETTING	COOKING TIME
1 cup plums	200–300 ml	medium–high	2 mins
2 cups plums	350–450 ml	medium–high	3 mins
3 cups plums	550–650 ml	medium–high	5 mins

(Note: For every additional jar add 1 minute's cooking time.)

6
Cool and store as directed on pages 10–11.

Tomatoes

METHOD

1

Tomatoes may be peeled by immersing them in boiling water for 2– 3 minutes first. The skins will then come away easily.

2

Place in clean, sterilised jars.

3

Fit lids according to instructions on page 9.

4

Cook as follows:

FRUIT	JAR SIZE	OVEN SETTING	COOKING TIME
1 tomato	200–300 ml	medium–high	2 mins
2 tomatoes	350–450 ml	medium–high	3 mins
3 tomatoes	550–650 ml	medium–high	5 mins

(Note: For every additional jar add 1 minute's cooking time.)

5

Cool for 12 hours then repeat step 4 without loosening screw-on lids or removing spring clips.

6

Cool again and store as directed on pages 10–11.

~ TOMATOES ~

TWO FRUITS

METHOD

1

Selection of fruits is important. Fruits low in natural acids are not recommended, e.g. bananas, cantaloupe, pawpaw, figs and mangoes. Suggested combinations of fruits are:

- peaches and pears
- peaches and apricots
- apricots and pears
- pineapple and apricots
- berries and diced apple
- apple and quince.

2

Peel, stone or core and prepare fruit as appropriate, e.g. dice, slice or ball. Add sweetener if desired.

3

Place in clean, sterilised jars, alternating layers for visual effect.

4

Fit lids according to instructions on page 9.

5

Cook as follows:

FRUIT	JAR SIZE	OVEN SETTING	COOKING TIME
1 cup fruit	200–300 ml	medium-high	2 mins
2 cups fruit	350–450 ml	medium-high	3 mins
3 cups fruit	550–650 ml	medium-high	5 mins

(Note: For every additional jar add 1 minute's cooking time.)

6

Cool and store as directed on pages 10–11.

2

LOW-SUGAR WHOLE-FRUIT JAMS

Many of us find jam too sweet for the taste buds or too high in calories for the waistline. The following recipes use only half to a quarter of the amount of sugar in conventional recipes, resulting in a fuller, fruitier jam that is better for you. Again, as microwave cooking draws out the natural juices, no water is needed. The fruit is therefore more concentrated and less sugar is needed for setting.

In this new method of jam-making, the whole fruit is used, with the sweetener of your choice.

Setting point

It is essential to test mixtures to make sure that setting point has been reached, otherwise the flavour, texture and colour of the product will be spoilt, making it unusable. In all jam-making setting point is checked as follows:

1 Before preparing fruit, place an empty saucer in the refrigerator.

2 Remove bowl of cooked fruit from oven. (If you continue heating fruit while testing the sample, it may cook beyond setting point.)

3 Put a teaspoon of hot mixture on the cold saucer and let stand. When cool, the surface should crinkle when saucer is tilted slightly.

4 If test is negative, return bowl to oven and cook on HIGH for a few more minutes. Repeat test.

Warming the jars

To achieve the best results, warm the jars just before filling them with cooked jams or chutneys, as follows:

1 Cover bases of jars with water.

2 Place in microwave oven and cook on HIGH until water boils.

3 Pour off water just before filling jars.

Vacuum sealing jams

Vacuum sealing expels air from filled jars and seals them. While it is not essential to vacuum seal jams, the process will ensure the longest possible keeping time. Seal as follows:

1 Choose screw-top jars with built-in sealing rings.

2 After you fill the jars, lightly screw on their lids.

3 While filled jars are still hot, place them in oven, about 3 cm (1¼ in) apart and cook on MEDIUM–HIGH for 1–2 minutes. Remove jars from oven and place on a towel, several sheets of newspaper or a chopping board to prevent cracking. Screw lids down tightly, protecting your hands with an oven mitt or a towel, and let stand.

4 When cool, the lids will be slightly concave, showing that a vacuum seal has been achieved.

Storage

Store jams in a cool, dark place. This retards the growth of mould. If mould does form, remove and discard it. Place remaining mixture in a microwave-proof bowl and cook on HIGH at boiling point for 2–3 minutes. Re-bottle in clean, warm, sterilised jars and vacuum seal.

Pectin and fruit acids

Pectin, a naturally occurring fruit acid, is a vital element in jams, without which they would not set. The highest quantities of pectin occur in fruits that are firm and just under-ripe (pectin in over-ripe fruit converts to sugar).

Fruits with high levels of acid are ideal, as the acid inhibits the growth of bacteria and prevents the formation of toxins. Natural fruit acids are also necessary because they draw out pectin, improve the flavour of the fruit and help prevent crystallisation.

If the fruit is over-ripe or naturally low in pectin or other fruit acids, lemon juice or citric acid must be added. the amounts required are specified in the recipes.

HIGH-PECTIN FRUITS	MEDIUM-PECTIN FRUITS	LOW-PECTIN FRUITS
cooking apples	apricots	bananas
crab apples	blackberries	ripe cherries
quinces	under-ripe berries	figs
citrus fruits:	loganberries	grapes
cumquats	greengage plums	peaches
grapefruit	ripe plums	pears
lemons	pineapples	strawberries
oranges	rhubarb	

Testing Pectin Content

Place a teaspoon of cooked or preserved fruit in 3 teaspoons of methylated spirits and leave for 2 minutes until mixture clots and becomes firm.

Large, firm clots indicate high pectin content. Medium-sized clots that are not so firm indicate medium pectin content. Weak, flabby clots indicate low pectin content.

Overcoming Pectin Deficiency

Sweet, over-ripe fruit and fruits low in pectin can be used in jams if one of the following steps is taken:

1 Add 2 tablespoons of lemon juice to every kilogram (4 cups) of fruit.

2 Add 1 teaspoon of citric acid to every kilogram (4 cups) of fruit.

3 Add commercially produced pectin, following the manufacturer's instructions.

LOW-SUGAR WHOLE-FRUIT JAM

As all jam depends on a minimum quantity of sugar to set, it is not possible to make sugar-free jam. However, good results can be achieved using half or a quarter of the quantity of sweetener in conventional jams. On the opposite page is the basic recipe for such jams. See pages 36-42 for proportionate quantities of fruit and sweetener.

Using half the sweetener

The jams in this chapter use half the quantity of sweetener of that in conventional jam recipes. Note that the sweeteners listed are alternatives to each other.

Using quarter the sweetener

If you want to use only quarter the quantity of sweetener used in conventional jam recipes, halve again the amount used in the following recipes. Note that the sweeteners listed are alternatives.

METHOD

1
Choose firm, unblemished fruit which is slightly under-ripe. Cut away and discard any bruised areas.

2
Wash fruit, peel if necessary, cut into halves and remove any pips or stones.

3
Add lemon juice or citric acid if required.

4
Place fruit mixture in a covered microwave-proof bowl, cook on HIGH until soft and pulpy.

5
Remove bowl from oven and stir in required amount of sweetener (see following recipes in this chapter) while pulp is still hot, and making sure it dissolves.

6
Return mixture to microwave and cook uncovered on HIGH for approximately 15-20 minutes, until setting point has been reached (see page 31).

7
Skim jam to remove any scum.

8
Fill clean, warm, sterilised jars to the brim.

9
Vacuum seal according to directions on pages 31–32.

10
Label and date jars.

11
Cool and store as directed on pages 10–11.

APPLE & BLACKBERRY JAM

INGREDIENTS
Cooking apples, 1 kg (2 lb)
Blackberries, 1 kg (2 lb)
Honey, 1 kg (3 cups)
or
Golden syrup, 1 kg (3 cups)
or
Brown or white sugar, 1 kg (2 lb)
Lemon juice, 2 tablespoons
or
Citric acid, 1 teaspoon

METHOD

Follow directions on page 35.

APPLE & RHUBARB JAM

INGREDIENTS
Cooking apples, 500 g (1 lb)
Rhubarb, 500 g (1 lb)
Honey, 500 g (1½ cups)
or
Golden syrup, 500 g (1½ cups)
or
Brown or white sugar, 500 g (1 lb)
Lemon juice, 2 tablespoons
or
Citric acid, 1 teaspoon

METHOD

Follow directions on page 35.

APRICOT JAM

INGREDIENTS
Apricots, 1 kg (2 lb)
Honey, 500 g (1½ cups)
or
Golden syrup, 500 g (1½ cups)
or
Brown or white sugar, 500 g (1 lb)

METHOD

Follow directions on page 35.

APRICOT & PINEAPPLE JAM

INGREDIENTS
Apricots, 1 kg (2 lb)
Drained crushed pineapple, 2 cups
Honey, 575 g (1¾ cups)
or
Golden syrup, 575 g (1¾ cups)
or
Brown or white sugar, 575 g (1 lb 2 oz)

METHOD

Follow directions on page 35.

~ BLACKBERRIES ~

BERRY JAM

INGREDIENTS
Raspberries, 1 kg (2 lb)
or
Blackberries, 1 kg (2 lb)
or
Strawberries, 1 kg (2 lb)
Honey, 500 g (1½ cups)
or
Golden syrup, 500 g (1½ cups)
or
Brown or white sugar, 500 g (1 lb)
Lemon juice, 2 tablespoons
or
Citric acid, 1 teaspoon

METHOD

Follow directions on page 35.

CHERRY JAM

Cherries, 1 kg (2 lb)
Honey, 500 g (1½ cups)
or
Golden syrup, 500 g (1½ cups)
or
Brown or white sugar, 500 g (1 lb)
Lemon juice, 2 tablespoons
or
Citric acid, 1 teaspoon

METHOD

Follow directions on page 35.

FIG JAM

Figs, 1 kg (2 lb)
Honey, 500 g (1½ cups)
or
Golden syrup, 500 g (1½ cups)
or
Brown or white sugar, 500 g (1 lb)
Lemon juice, 2 tablespoons
or
Citric acid, 1 teaspoon

METHOD

Follow directions on page 35.

FIG & GINGER JAM

INGREDIENTS
Figs, 2 kg (4 lb)
Fresh green ginger, bruised, 90 g (3 oz)
Honey, 1 kg (3 cups)
or
Golden syrup, 1 kg (3 cups)
or
Brown or white sugar, 1 kg (2 lb)
Lemon juice, 3 tablespoons
or
Citric acid, 1½ teaspoons

METHOD

Follow directions on page 35.

MANGO & PINEAPPLE JAM

INGREDIENTS
Mangoes, 1 kg (2 lb)
Diced fresh pineapple, 2 cups
Thinly sliced lemon, 1
Honey, 500 g (1½ cups)
or
Golden syrup, 500 g (1½ cups)
or
Brown or white sugar, 500 g (1 lb)

METHOD

Follow directions on page 35.

MELON & GINGER JAM

INGREDIENTS
Jam melon, peeled, diced and seeded, 2 kg (4 lb)
(Leave diced melon to stand overnight to extract excess liquid. Pour this away before making jam.)
Fresh green ginger, bruised, 60 g (2 oz)
Honey, 1 kg (3 cups)
or
Golden syrup, 1 kg (3 cups)
or
Brown or white sugar, 1 kg (2 lb)
Lemon juice, 3 tablespoons
or
Citric acid, 1½ teaspoons

METHOD

Follow directions on page 35.

PEACH JAM

INGREDIENTS
Clingstone peaches, 2 kg (4 lb)
Honey, 1 kg (3 cups)
or
Golden syrup, 1 kg (3 cups)
or
Brown or white sugar, 1 kg (2 lb)
Lemon juice, 3 tablespoons
or
Citric acid, 1 ½ teaspoons

METHOD

Follow directions on page 35.

PEAR & GINGER JAM

INGREDIENTS
Pears, 2 kg (4 lb)
Fresh green ginger, bruised, 60 g (2 oz)
Honey, 1 kg (3 cups)
or
Golden syrup, 1 kg (3 cups)
or
Brown or white sugar, 1 kg (2 lb)
Lemon juice, 3 tablespoons
or
Citric acid, 1½ teaspoons

METHOD

Follow directions on page 35.

PINEAPPLE JAM

Pineapple, 1 kg (2 lb)
Honey, 500 g (1½ cups)
or
Golden syrup, 500 g (1½ cups)
or
Brown or white sugar, 500 g (1 lb)
Lemon juice, 2 tablespoons
or
Citric acid, 1 teaspoon

METHOD

Follow directions on page 35.

PLUM JAM

INGREDIENTS
Plums, 2 kg (4 lb)
Honey, 1 kg (3 cups)
or
Golden syrup, 1 kg (3 cups)
or
Brown or white sugar, 1 kg (2 lb)

METHOD

Follow directions on page 35.

3

SAVOURY SAUCES

So many dishes can be transformed or greatly enhanced by an appropriate sauce.

Some sauces are made with the meal and served immediately. Others can be bottled and stored ready for any occasion. All recipes given here use considerably less than the traditional amount of sugar.

Vacuum sealing sauces

If directed by the recipe, vacuum seal according to instructions for jam (page 32), but use the cooking times below. These apply to one jar only. For every additional jar add 1 minute's extra cooking time.

JAR SIZE	OVEN SETTING	COOKING TIME
250–350 ml	MEDIUM-HIGH	2 mins
400–650 ml	MEDIUM-HIGH	3 mins
700–900 ml	MEDIUM-HIGH	4 mins

CUMBERLAND SAUCE

INGREDIENTS
Orange, 1
Lemon, 1
Sugar, 4 tablespoons
Port wine, 4 tablespoons
Cornflour, 2 teaspoons
blended with
Water, 2 teaspoons

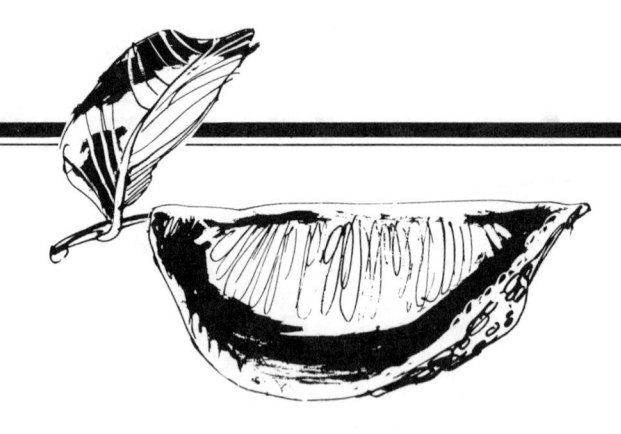

METHOD

1
Peel the rind thinly from the orange and lemon and cut into fine strips.

2
Place in a microwave-proof bowl and cover with ½ cup water. Cook on HIGH for 3–4 minutes. Set aside.

3
Squeeze juice from both fruits and heat on high for 30–60 seconds.

4
Quickly stir in sugar to dissolve. Cook on HIGH for a further 2–3 minutes.

5
Add port, blended cornflour. Cook to thicken.

6
Drain water from cooked rind and stir into sauce.

7
While still hot, fill clean, sterilised jars, fit lids, store.

8
Vacuum seal for longer storage life (see page 43).

Note: If sauce has been allowed to cool, add 1 minute to specified sealing times.

9
Label and date jars. *Serve with ham or lamb.*

Fresh fruit can be preserved in minutes, pages 6-29.

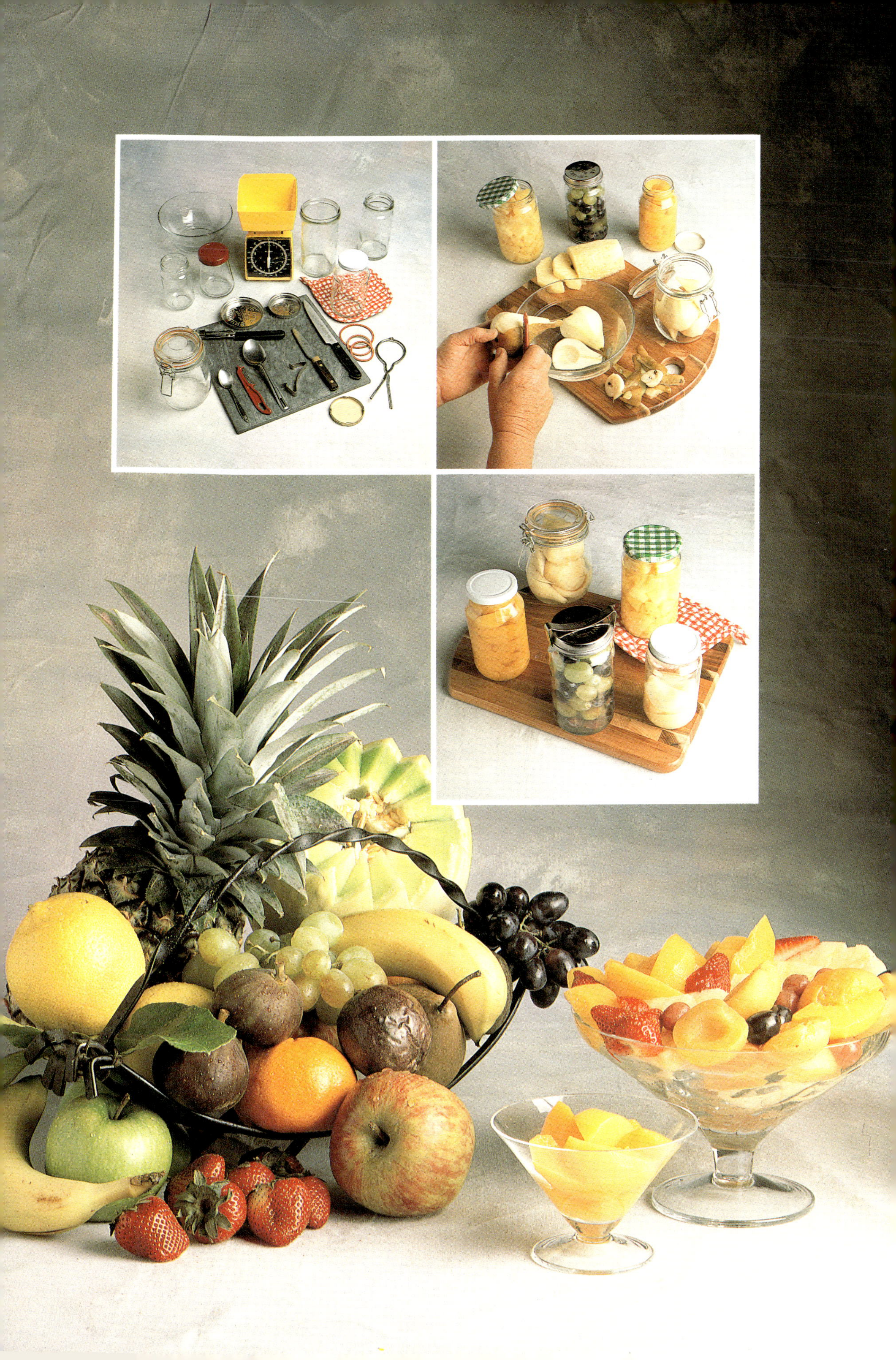

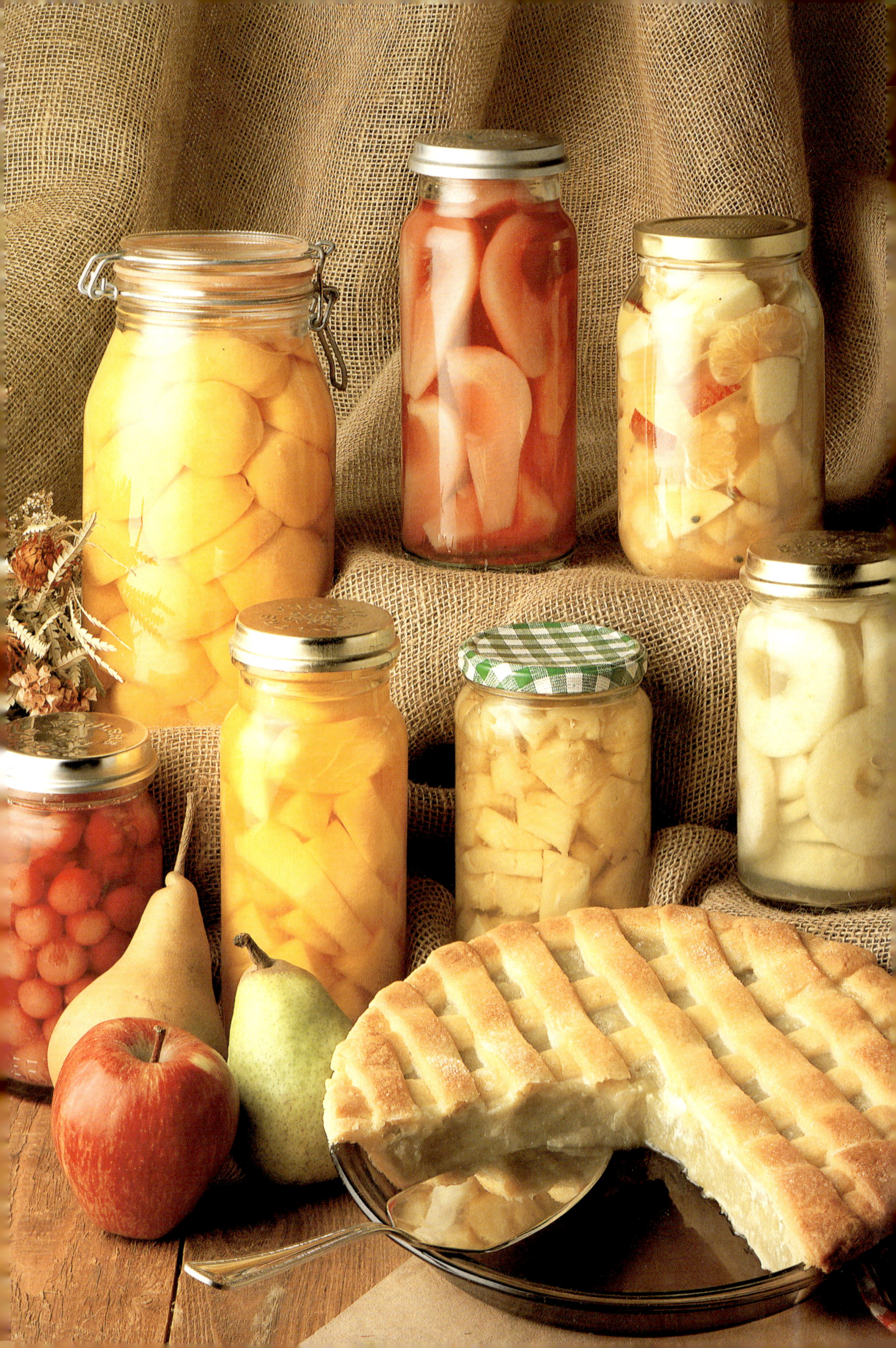

CURRY SAUCE

INGREDIENTS
Cooking apples, 2
Onions, 2 (medium)
Curry powder, 3 tablespoons
Plain flour, 60 g (2 oz)
Water or beef stock, 1 litre (4 cups)
Sweet chutney, 3 tablespoons
Tomato paste, 2 tablespoons
Cooking oil, 2 tablespoons
Juice of ½ lemon

METHOD

1
Peel, core and dice apples.

2
Stir curry powder into ½ cup of stock and allow to stand at least 10 minutes. This is for added flavour.

3
Blend flour into curry mixture.

4
Place all ingredients into a large covered, microwave-proof bowl and cook on MEDIUM-HIGH for 20-25 minutes.

5
While still hot, fill clean, sterilised jars, fit lids, store.

6
Vacuum seal for longer storage life (see page 43).

Note: If sauce has been allowed to cool, add 1 minute to specified sealing times.

7
Label and date jars.

Bottled fruit makes a wholesome, delicious dessert.

Horseradish Sauce

INGREDIENTS
Horseradish root, grated, ½ cup
Vinegar, 1 tablespoon
Sugar, 2 tablespoons
Cream, 1 tablespoon
Plain yoghurt, 1 cup

METHOD

1
Place horseradish, vinegar and sugar in a microwave-proof bowl and heat on HIGH for 30–60 seconds.

2
Stir to dissolve sugar. Allow to cool.

3
Stir in cream and yoghurt.

4
Allow to stand 2-3 hours before serving with beef, or keep in an airtight jar in refrigerator for up to 2 weeks.

Tomato Sauce

INGREDIENTS
Ripe tomatoes, 2 kg (4 lb)
Brown onions, 500 g (1 lb)
Sugar, 375 g (12 oz)
Salt, 30 g (1 oz)
Spiced vinegar, ¾ cup (See page 54)

METHOD

1
Chop tomatoes and onions roughly.

2
Cook in a large microwave-proof bowl until tender (approximately 20–25 minutes).

3
Pour away approximately ½ of the tomato liquid (this can be used in soups, casseroles, etc.)

4
Puree tomatoes and onions in a food processor or blender, strain off skins and seeds and return to bowl.

5
Stir in sugar, salt and spiced vinegar.

6
Heat to boiling point on HIGH, stirring to dissolve sugar. Continue boiling until sauce has thickened, approximately 20–30 minutes. Stir 2 or 3 times during this cooking period.

7
Allow to cool for approximately 10 minutes.

8
Fill clean, warm, sterilised jars or bottles, seal with lid and store in a cool cupboard.

No-Tears Tomato Sauce

INGREDIENTS
Ripe tomatoes, 2 kg (4 lb)
Cooking apple, 1
Crushed garlic, 1 good tablespoon
Sugar, 375 g (12 oz)
Salt, 30 g (1 oz)
Spiced vinegar, ¾ cup (See page 54)

METHOD

1
Chop tomatoes and apple roughly.

2
Cook in a large microwave-proof bowl until tender (approximately 20–25 minutes).

3
Pour away approximately ½ of the tomato liquid (this can be used in soups, casseroles, etc.)

4
Puree tomatoes and apple in a food processor or blender, strain off skins and seeds and return to bowl.

5
Stir in sugar, salt and spiced vinegar.

6
Heat to boiling point on HIGH. Stir to dissolve sugar. Continue boiling until sauce has thickened, approximately 20–30 minutes. Stir 2 or 3 times during this cooking period.

7
Allow to cool for approximately 10 minutes.

8
Fill clean, warm, sterilised jars or bottles, seal with lid and store in a cool cupboard.

BARBECUE SAUCE

INGREDIENTS
Tomato sauce, 2 cups
Worcestershire sauce, 1/3 cup
Brown vinegar, 1/3 cup
Garlic, crushed, 1 tablespoon
Prepared mustard, 1 teaspoon

METHOD

1

Place all ingredients in a microwave-proof bowl and stir together.

2

Cook on HIGH for 3–4 minutes.

3

Fill clean, warm, sterilised jar, seal with lid and store in a cool cupboard.

Great with barbecue sausages.

TARTARE SAUCE

INGREDIENTS
Mayonnaise, 1 cup
White vinegar, 1 tablespoon
Gherkins, chopped, 1 tablespoon
Capers, chopped, 1 teaspoon (optional)
Mustard powder, 1 teaspoon
Pinch mixed herbs

METHOD

1

Place all ingredients in a heat-resistant microwave-proof bowl and stir together.

2
Heat on MEDIUM–HIGH for 1 minute. Do not allow sauce to boil.

3
Place in clean, warm, sterilised jar, seal with lid and refrigerate. Will keep 1–2 months.

This sauce complements fish very well.

APPLE SAUCE

INGREDIENTS
Cooking apples, 3–4
Butter, 30 g (1 oz)
Water, 1 cup
Squeeze of lemon juice
Sugar to taste

METHOD

1
Peel, core and dice apples.

2
Cook apples and water in a heat-resistant microwave-proof bowl on HIGH until tender, approximately 6–10 minutes.

3
Mash apples to a puree with a fork or a blender.

4
Before serving, stir in butter, lemon juice and sugar to taste.

5
Can be stored in airtight jar in the refrigerator for 1–2 weeks.

Serve with roast pork.

Plum Sauce

INGREDIENTS
Blood plums, 2 kg (4 lb)
Sugar, 500 g (1 lb)
Salt, 10 g (2 teaspoons)
Allspice, 5 g (1 teaspoon)
Cloves, 5 g (1 teaspoon)
Vinegar, 2 cups
Cayenne pepper, ½ tablespoon
Fresh green ginger, bruised, 1 small piece

METHOD

1
Wash plums well and remove stems.

2
Place all ingredients in a microwave-proof bowl.

3
Cook on HIGH for about 18-25 minutes or until fruit is very soft. Cool. Remove stones.

4
Puree in a food processor or blender, then strain off skins.

5
Fill clean, warm, sterilised jars or bottles, seal with lid and store in a cool cupboard.

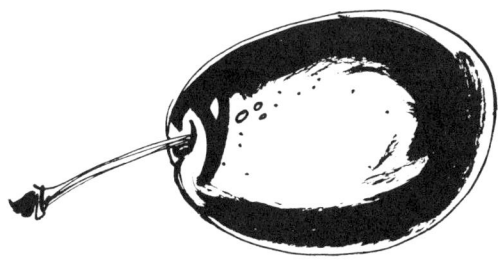

~ PLUM ~

Tomato Plum Sauce

INGREDIENTS
Ripe tomatoes, 1 kg (2 lb)
Ripe plums, 1 kg (2 lb)
Sugar, 500 g (1 lb)
Vinegar, 400 ml (1½ cups)
Salt, 5 g (1 teaspoon)
Mixed spice, 5 g (1 teaspoon)
Cayenne pepper, ½ teaspoon
Ginger, fresh (crushed or bruised), 30g (1 oz)
or
Ginger (ground), 1 teaspoon

METHOD

1
Cut up all fruit roughly and place in a microwave-proof bowl with all other ingredients.

2
Cook on HIGH for approximately 10–12 minutes.

3
Stir to dissolve sugar, then boil on HIGH for 30–40 minutes, or until sauce has thickened.

4
Allow to cool slightly and remove plum stones.

5
Puree in a food processor or blender to a smooth sauce consistency.

6
Fill clean, warm, sterilised bottle, seal with lid.

7
Vacuum seal for longer storage life (see page 43).

4

CHUTNEYS, RELISHES AND PICKLES

The versatility of chutneys and relishes is endless, as the combination of different fruits and spices can be blended and adjusted to suit almost any dish or personal taste.

The secret of a good chutney is to store it for 6–8 weeks before use, allowing the flavours to blend and mature.

Chutneys and relishes give you the opportunity to use blemished fruits or those that are too ripe for bottling or jams. Do cut away all blemishes or damage before using, though, as they can still cause contamination.

Chutneys, relishes and pickles do not need to be vacuum sealed. To prevent drying out and shrinking during storage, cover with a screw top rather than jam covers or paper, so that the vinegar does not evaporate.

Vinegar

Use high-quality vinegar in chutneys and pickles. Brown malt vinegar is the usual choice, but wine vinegar can also be used for its special flavour. White malt or cider vinegar are used for pickling light-coloured vegetables.

Commercially produced spiced vinegar can be used, but a wider variety of flavours is possible if you prepare your own, as follows:

Spiced Vinegar

INGREDIENTS
Vinegar, 1 litre
Whole cloves, 1 teaspoon
Black peppercorns, 2 teaspoons
Bay leaves, 2–3
Cinnamon stick, 5 cm (2 in)
Mustard seed, 1 teaspoon

METHOD

Place all ingredients in a microwave-proof bowl. Bring liquid to boil, approximately 5 minutes. Remove from oven and allow to cool. Strain and store in clean bottles ready for use.

~ALLSPICE~

Spices

Whole spices should be used for pickles, as ground spices will make the vinegar cloudy. However, ground spices should be used for chutneys, as they give a stronger flavour. If you use whole spices for chutneys, add more than the amount stated in the recipe and tie them in a muslin bag. The bag can be removed easily before the chutney is bottled.

Brine

For best results use coarse cooking salt, as refined table salt produces a cloudy effect. The ideal solution for soaked vegetables is 125 grams (½ cup) of salt to 2 litres (8 cups) of water. Dissolve the salt in boiling water and cool. Strain the brine before using it, and carefully rinse all traces of it from the vegetables before soaking them in the spiced vinegar.

Sugar

Chutneys are usually sweetened with white granulated sugar, but brown sugar can be used to make chutneys darker and alter their flavour. Note, however, that a darker chutney can be achieved simply by cooking the mixture for a longer period.

APPLE & DATE CHUTNEY

INGREDIENTS
Cooking apples, peeled, cored and diced, 4 (medium)
Seeded dates, chopped, 1 cup
Chilli powder, 1 teaspoon
Honey or golden syrup, 1 cup
Brown vinegar, 2 cups
Allspice, ground, ¼ teaspoon
Cloves, whole, 6
Salt, 1 tablespoon
Onions, 2 (large)
Raisins or sultanas, 1 cup

METHOD

1
Place all ingredients in a large microwave-proof bowl.

2
Cook on HIGH until boiling (about 8–10 minutes).

3
Stir to dissolve sugar.

4
Cook on HIGH for 40–45 minutes or until chutney has thickened.

5
Fill clean, warm jars. Seal with lid while still hot.

6
Store in a cool cupboard for at least 1 week before serving.

APPLE & GINGER CHUTNEY

INGREDIENTS
Cooking apples, 1 kg (2 lb)
Green ginger, 90 g (3 oz)
White vinegar, 1 cup
Brown sugar, 180 g (1½ cups)
Allspice, ground, ½ teaspoon
Salt, ½ teaspoon
Onion, 1 (medium)
Capsicum, 1
Sultanas, ½ cup
Lemon rind, 1 tablespoon

METHOD

1
Peel, core and dice apples, onion and capsicum.

2
Peel ginger and crush or chop finely.

3
Place all ingredients in a heat-resistant microwave-proof bowl.

4
Cook on HIGH until boiling, approximately 6–8 minutes.

5
Stir to dissolve sugar.

6
Continue cooking on HIGH until chutney has thickened, approximately 15–20 minutes.

7
Fill clean, warm jars. Seal with lid while still hot. Store in a cool cupboard.

Hot Choko Relish

INGREDIENTS
Chokos, 4
Onions, 3 (medium)
Cooking apples, 3 (large)
Sultanas, ½ cup
Raisins, ½ cup
Brown sugar, 1½ cups
Vinegar, 1½ cups
Prepared mustard, 2 teaspoons
Turmeric, 2 teaspoons
Cayenne pepper, 1 teaspoon
Curry powder, 1 teaspoon
Garlic, 1 clove, crushed
Salt, ½ teaspoon

METHOD

1
Peel chokos, onions and apples and remove cores.

2
Dice and place in a large microwave-proof bowl along with all other ingredients.

3
Cook on HIGH until boiling.

4
Stir once to dissolve sugar.

5
Cook on HIGH for 30–35 minutes or until relish has thickened.

6
Fill clean, warm jars. Seal with lids while still hot.

7
Cool and store in a cool cupboard.

PICKLED GHERKINS

INGREDIENTS
Gherkins
Spiced vinegar (See page 54)

METHOD

1
Soak gherkins in brine (see page 55) for 3 days.

2
Drain well and dry.

3
Pack gherkins carefully into jars.

4
Bring spiced vinegar to the boil on HIGH.

5
Pour over gherkins till they are covered. Screw on lid and leave for 24 hours.

6
Strain vinegar from gherkins and reheat on HIGH till boiling.

7
Pour over gherkins till they are covered. Screw on lid and leave for another 24 hours.

8
Repeat steps 6 and 7 until gherkins are a good green colour.

9
Before storing, ensure that gherkins are well covered with vinegar.

RED TOMATO CHUTNEY

INGREDIENTS
Ripe tomatoes, 1 kg (2 lb)
Cooking apples, 2 (large)
Onions, 250 g (½ lb)
Sultanas, ½ cup
Raisins, ½ cup
Brown sugar, 250 g (½ lb)
Vinegar, 1 cup
Prepared mustard, 1 teaspoon
Allspice, ground, 1 teaspoon
Salt, 1 teaspoon

METHOD

1
Peel tomatoes and onions and cut up roughly. Peel, core and dice apples.

2
Place all ingredients in a large microwave-proof bowl.

3
Cook on HIGH until boiling, approximately 6–8 minutes.

4
Stir to dissolve sugar.

5
Continue cooking on HIGH until chutney has thickened, approximately 18–20 minutes.

6
Fill clean, warm jars. Seal with lid while still hot. Store in a cool cupboard.

Keep a well-stocked larder of sauces, pages 43-52, chutneys and pickles, pages 53-64.

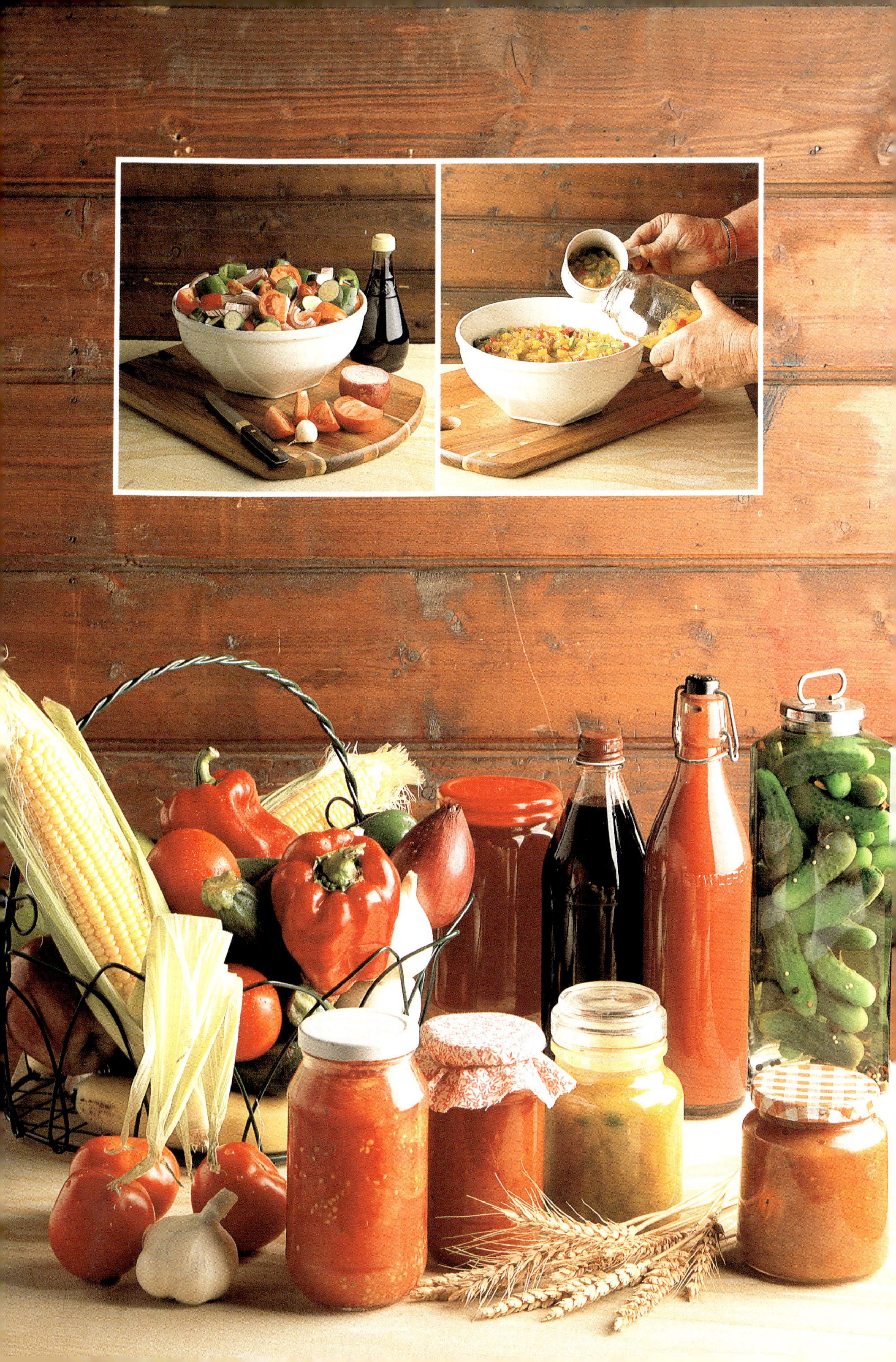

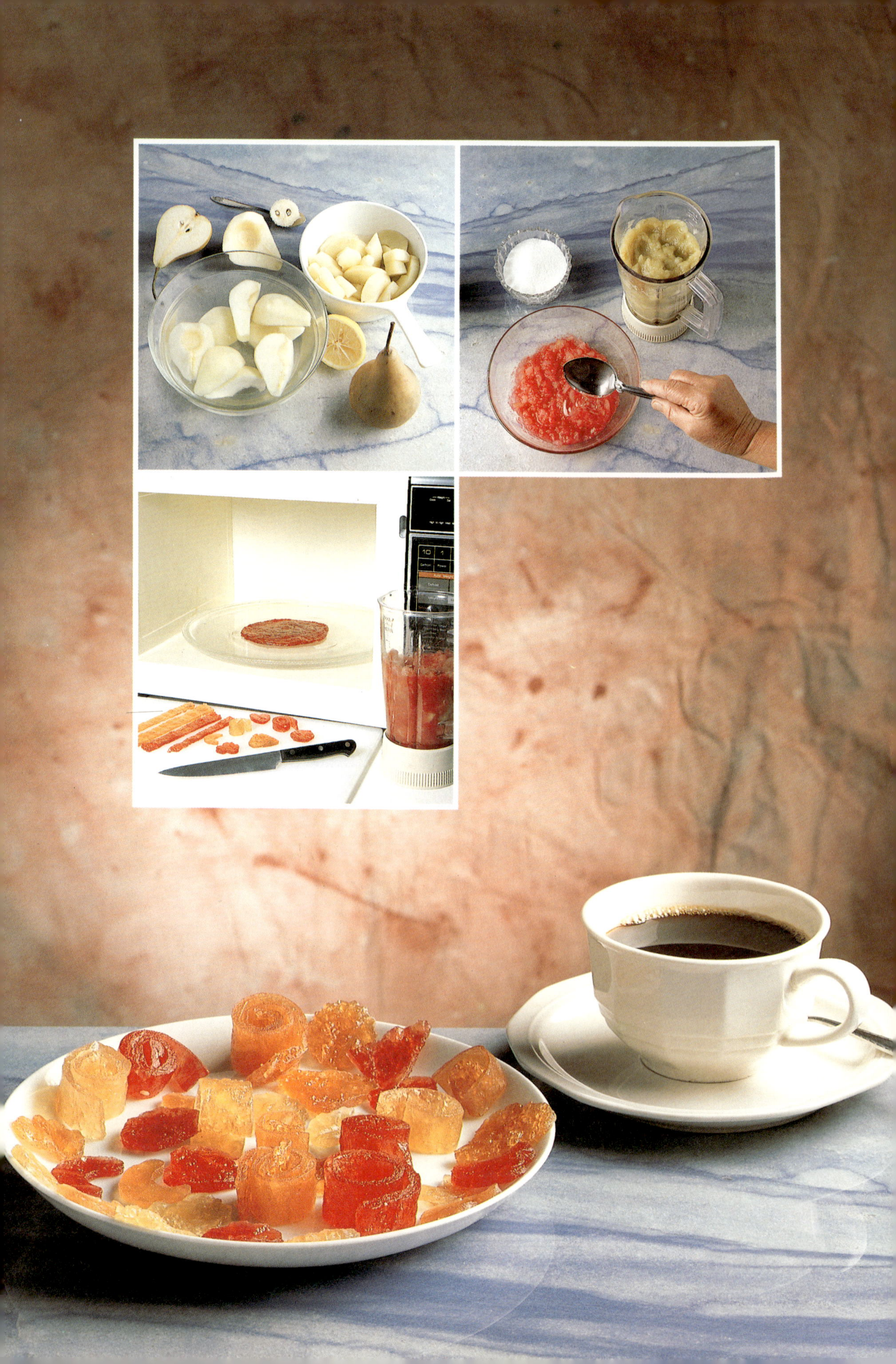

RHUBARB CHUTNEY

INGREDIENTS
Rhubarb, 1 kg (2 lb)
Onions, 2
Garlic, 1 clove, crushed
Salt, 1 teaspoon
Mixed spice, 1 teaspoon
Sugar, 250 g (½ lb)
Vinegar, 250 ml (1 cup)

METHOD

1
Remove leaves, base and outer skin or string from rhubarb. Cut into 2.5-cm (1 in) pieces.

2
Peel onions and dice finely.

3
Place all ingredients in a large microwave-proof bowl.

4
Bring to boil on HIGH.

5
Stir to dissolve sugar.

6
Continue cooking on HIGH for approximately 12–15 minutes or until chutney has thickened.

7
Fill clean, warm jars. Seal with lid while still hot.

8
Store in a cool cupboard.

Make fruit roll-ups the easy way, pages 85-87.

Sweetcorn Relish

INGREDIENTS
Cornflour, 1 tablespoon
Capsicums, 1 red & 1 green
Sweetcorn kernels, 375 g
Onion, 1 (large)
Sugar, 1/3 cup
White wine vinegar, 1 cup
Prepared mustard, 1 tablespoon
Turmeric, 2 teaspoons
White or black pepper, ground, 1 teaspoon
Garlic, 1 clove, crushed
Vegetable oil, 1 tablespoon

METHOD

1
Blend cornflour with a little of the vinegar until smooth. Dice capsicums, discarding cores, seeds and pith. Set aside.

2
Heat oil in a large bowl on HIGH for 1 minute.

3
Add capsicum, corn, onion, garlic, sugar, turmeric, mustard and 1 cup vinegar. Stir to mix.

4
Cook on HIGH for 4 minutes. Stir then add pepper.

5
Stir in blended cornflour and heat on HIGH till boiling.

6
Bottle and seal.

7
Store in a cool, dark cupboard ready for use.

ZUCCHINI PICKLES

INGREDIENTS
Zucchini, 1 kg (2 lb)
Green tomatoes, 1 kg (2 lb)
Onions, 2 (large)
Cucumbers, 2 (large)
Salt, 3 tablespoons
Brown vinegar, 750 ml (3 cups)
Sugar, 500 g (1 lb)

Bouquet garni:
Mix together in gauze tied to form a small bag
Chilli powder, ½ teaspoon
Cayenne pepper, ¼ teaspoon
Cloves, ground, ½ teaspoon
Whole allspice, ½ teaspoon
Whole black peppercorns, ½ teaspoon

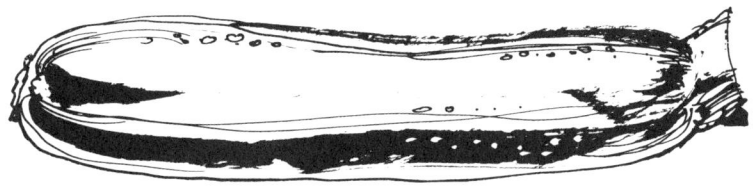

~CHILLI~

~ONIONS & ZUCCHINI~

To make paste:
Mix together
Cornflour, 2 tablespoons
Mustard powder, 1 tablespoon
Turmeric, 1 dessertspoon
Water, ½ cup

METHOD

1
Cut all vegetables into small pieces. (Skin can be removed from the zucchini, or left on.)

2
Place all prepared vegetables in a large glass or plastic bowl.

3
Sprinkle with salt and allow to stand overnight.

4
Next day, pour away liquid, add vinegar, sugar and *bouquet garni* to vegetables and cook on HIGH for 20–40 minutes.

5
While still hot, thicken with prepared paste.

6
Cook a further 3–4 minutes or until mixture is clear.

7
Bottle and seal.

8
Store in a cool, dark cupboard ready for use.

~TURMERIC ROOT~

5

FRUIT AND NUT BUTTERS

Fruit butters make a welcome change from the usual jams, and are especially popular with sweet-toothed children.

Once sealed in the jar, these butters will keep for several weeks in a cool, dark cupboard.

APPLE BUTTER

INGREDIENTS
Cooking apples, 1 kg (2 lb)
Water, 1 cup
Lemon juice, 2 tablespoons
Sugar, ½ cup
Cinnamon, 1 dessertspoon
Cloves, ground, ¼ teaspoon

METHOD

1
Place washed, roughly cut-up apples (retaining skins and cores) in a microwave-proof bowl. Add water and lemon juice.

2
Cook on HIGH for approximately 8-10 minutes or until apples are soft.

3
Puree in a food processor or blender.

4
Return apples to a microwave-proof bowl and add sugar and spices.

5
Cook on HIGH for approximately 6–8 minutes or until mixture has thickened and holds its shape when tested on a cold plate.

6
Fill clean, sterilised jars. Secure lids.

7
Vacuum seal as directed on page 32.

APRICOT BUTTER

INGREDIENTS
Apricots, 1 kg (2 lb)
Sugar, ½ cup
Water, ½ cup
Pinch nutmeg
Cinnamon, ½ teaspoon

METHOD

1
Halve apricots and remove stones. Add water.

2
Cook on HIGH for approximately 8–10 minutes or until apricots are soft.

3
Puree in a food processor or blender.

4
Return apricots to a microwave-proof bowl and add sugar and spices.

5
Cook on HIGH for approximately 6-8 minutes or until mixture has thickened and holds its shape when tested on a cold plate.

6
Fill clean, sterilised jars. Secure lids.

7
Vacuum seal as directed on page 32.

CRUNCHY PEANUT BUTTER

INGREDIENTS
Unsalted roasted peanuts, 500 g (1 lb)
Salt, ½ teaspoon
Cooking oil, ¼–½ cup

METHOD

1
Remove husks, if any, by spreading peanuts evenly over carousel plate. Cook on HIGH for 2-3 minutes or until husks rub off easily. Discard.

2
Crush half the peanuts in a food processor until they are small pieces. Remove.

3
Blend the remaining peanuts with oil to a smooth paste, then add the crushed peanuts and blend until just mixed.

4
Fill clean, sterilised jars to 12 mm from lip.

5
Release any air from jar by sliding a knife or packing stick into air pockets.

6
Fit screw-on lids with built-in seals.

7
Cook as follows:

JAR SIZE	OVEN SETTING	COOKING TIME
250–350 ml	medium–high	2 mins
400–650 ml	medium–high	3 mins
700–900 ml	medium–high	4 mins

8
Cool, and store in a dark cupboard.

Very popular with kids.

LEMON BUTTER

INGREDIENTS
Rind and juice of 2 lemons
Butter, 60 g (2 oz)
Sugar, 125 g (4 oz)
Eggs, 2 (large), beaten

METHOD

1
Mix all ingredients in a microwave-proof bowl.

2
Cook on MEDIUM–HIGH for 6–8 minutes or until butter has thickened, stirring once to dissolve sugar during this cooking time.

3
Fill clean, sterilised jars. Secure lids.

4
Vacuum seal as directed on page 32.

ORANGE BUTTER

INGREDIENTS
Rind and juice of 2 oranges
Butter, 60 g (2 oz)
Sugar, 125 g (4 oz)
Eggs, 2 (large), beaten

METHOD

1
Mix all ingredients in a microwave-proof bowl.

2
Cook on MEDIUM–HIGH for 6–8 minutes or until butter has thickened.

3
Fill clean, sterilised jars. Secure lids.

4
Vacuum seal as directed on page 32.

PASSIONFRUIT BUTTER

INGREDIENTS
Pulp of 8 passionfruit
Butter, 60 g (2 oz)
Sugar, 125 g (4 oz)
Eggs, 2 (large), beaten

METHOD

1
Mix all ingredients in a microwave-proof bowl.

2
Cook on MEDIUM–HIGH for 6–8 minutes or until butter has thickened.

3
Fill clean, sterilised jars. Secure lids.

4
Vacuum seal as directed on page 32.

~ PASSIONFRUIT ~

6

SUGARLESS FRUIT SPREADS

With the combination of microwave cooking and artificial sweeteners, it is now possible to produce a sugarless, jam-like spread. The spreads included here are simply fruit pulp to which an artificial sweetener is added when opened for use.

If artificial sweetener is cooked with the fruit it can result in a bitter aftertaste. The sweetener can be added to the fruit just before bottling or on serving. The latter is better, as you can adjust it to your taste buds.

Rather than trying to make large quantities of spreads when fresh fruit is available, you may find it easier to make smaller quantities of spreads from your sugarless 'just fruit' preserves throughout the year. This will give you greater variety.

~ PERSIMMON & FIG ~

NOTE: These spreads *must be vacuum sealed* for long keeping because without the assistance of sugar they will ferment within a few days. Use small jars so that the contents can be used up quickly after the seal is broken. Once opened, store the spreads in the refrigerator for up to 1 week.

BASIC FRUIT SPREADS

Ingredients and Cooking Times

SPREAD	INGREDIENTS	APPROXIMATE COOKING TIME (In Minutes)
Apple & raspberry	3 cooking apples 3 cups fresh raspberries	16–18
Apricot	24 apricots	14–16
Blackberry & plum	2 cups blackberries 8–10 blood plums	16–18
Blackberry	500 g (1 lb) blackberries	12–16
Banana & apple	1 banana 1 cooking apple juice of ½ lemon	5–8
Cherry & cantaloupe	500 g cherries 250 g cantaloupe juice of ½ lemon	15–18
Mango & banana	1 mango 1 banana juice of ½ lemon	6–8
Plum	1 kg cherry damson or blood plums	20–24
Plum & apple	500 g plums 500 g cooking apples	18–20

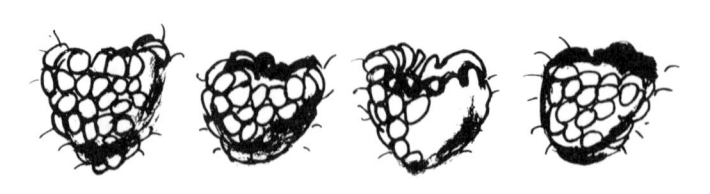

METHOD

1
Choose firm, unblemished fruit. Any bruising should be cut away and discarded.

2
Wash the fruit and peel it if necessary. Halve, and remove any pips or stones.

3
Place fruit in a large microwave-proof bowl. Cover.

4
Cook on HIGH until fruit is soft and pulpy.

5
Break up fruit with fork or potato masher or blender.

6
Return to oven (uncovered) and cook on HIGH until fruit is of a thick jam-like consistency.

7
Fill clean, sterilised jars to the brim.

8
Fit screw-on lid with sealing ring.

9
Vacuum seal by cooking on MEDIUM–HIGH for 1 minute, adding 30 seconds for each additional jar.

10
Store in a cool, dark cupboard.

11
On opening, add artificial sweetener to taste.

SUGARLESS PLUM CHUTNEY SPREAD

INGREDIENTS
Dark red or blue plums, 500 g (1 lb)
Cooking apples, 2 (medium)
Brown vinegar 125 ml (½ cup)
Onion, 1 (large)
Allspice, ½ teaspoon
Whole cloves, 3

METHOD

1
Wash plums and remove stones. Peel and core apples and chop roughly.

2
Dice onions and combine with plums, apples and vinegar.

3
Cook on HIGH in a microwave-proof bowl until tender, approximately 6–8 minutes.

4
Add allspice and cloves, boil on HIGH for another 3–4 minutes or until chutney has thickened.

5
Remove cloves if desired.

6
Fill clean, sterilised jars to the brim.

7
Fit screw-on lids with sealing ring.

8
Vacuum seal by cooking on MEDIUM–HIGH for 1 minute, adding 30 seconds for each additional jar.

9
Store in a cool, dark cupboard.
10
On opening, add artificial sweetener to taste.

SUGARLESS RED TOMATO CHUTNEY SPREAD

INGREDIENTS
Tomatoes, 500 g (1 lb)
Apple, 1 (medium), peeled and cored
Onion, 1 (medium), peeled
Green capsicum (small), 1
Garlic, 1 clove, crushed
Vinegar 60 ml (¼ cup)
Ginger, ground, ½ teaspoon
Salt, ½ teaspoon

METHOD

1
Coarsely chop tomatoes and dice onion, apple and capsicum, discarding peel, core and seeds.

2
Place all ingredients in a microwave-proof bowl and leave uncovered.

3
Cook on HIGH until mixture has thickened, approximately 10–12 minutes.

4
Fill clean, sterilised jars to the brim.

5
Fit screw-on lids with sealing ring.

6
Vacuum seal by cooking on MEDIUM–HIGH for 1 minute, adding 30 seconds for each additional jar.

7
Store in a cool, dark cupboard.

8
On opening, add artificial sweetener to taste.

7

FRUIT DRINKS AND CORDIALS

It is reassuring to know that your fruit drinks and cordials are fresh, full-flavoured and without additives.

The secret to good fruit drinks and cordials is to use well- ripened fruit. This is high in vitamins and natural juices and produces good flavour and colour.

Nectar is thicker than fruit drink as more fruit pulp is added. It can be used in various meat dishes or served with ice-cream.

The nectar and fruit juice recipes given here are suitable for all fruits other than citrus. The cordial recipes may seem to contain a lot of sugar, but remember that this is diluted with water before drinking.

FRUIT JUICE

INGREDIENTS
Well ripened fruit, 2 cups
(Suggestions: apples, apricots, berries, peaches, pineapple, plums.)
Water, 3 cups

METHOD

1
Cut fruit roughly and place in a microwave-proof bowl.

2
Add water. Cover.

3
Cook on HIGH until boiling, approximately 5–6 minutes.

4
Boil for 2 minutes. Cool.

5
Strain off juice and fill clean, sterilised bottles.

6
Fit screw-on lids with built-in seals.

7
Cook as follows:

JAR SIZE	OVEN SETTING	COOKING TIME
250–350 ml	medium–high	2 mins
400–650 ml	medium–high	3 mins
700–900 ml	medium–high	4 mins

(Note: For every additional jar add 1 minute's cooking time.)

8
Store in refrigerator or cool cupboard.

Sugar or artificial sweetener can be added if desired. The remaining fruit can be cooked further on HIGH to make a sugarless spread.

TOMATO JUICE

INGREDIENTS
Tomatoes, 1 kg (2 lb)
Sugar, 2 teaspoons
Water, 500 ml (2 cups)

METHOD

1
Choose well-ripened, unblemished tomatoes. Wash well.

2
Coarsely chop tomatoes.

3
Place all ingredients in a microwave-proof bowl.

4
Cook on HIGH until boiling. Stir, then continue boiling for 5–6 minutes.

5
Strain juice through a fine sieve or jelly bag to remove seeds, skin and pulp.

6
Fill clean, sterilised jars.

7
Fit screw-on lids with built-in seals.

8
Cook as follows:

JAR SIZE	OVEN SETTING	COOKING TIME
250–350 ml	medium–high	4 mins
400–650 ml	medium–high	6 mins
700–900 ml	medium–high	8 mins

(Note: For every additional jar used add 1 minute's cooking time.)

9
Store in refrigerator or cool cupboards.

This makes a delicious breakfast-time starter and can be flavoured with freshly ground black pepper and lemon juice or a dash of Worcestershire sauce.

Fruit Nectar

INGREDIENTS
Well-ripened fruit, 3 cups
(Suggestions: apples, apricots, berries, peaches, pineapple, plums.)
Water, 3 cups

METHOD

1
Place equal quantities of water and fruit in a microwave-proof bowl.

2
Cook on HIGH until tender.

3
Gently press through a coarse strainer to extract all juices and a little fruit pulp.

4
Fit screw-on lids with built-in seals.

5
Cook as follows:

JAR SIZE	OVEN SETTING	COOKING TIME
250–350 ml	medium–high	2 mins
400–650 ml	medium–high	3 mins
700–900 ml	medium–high	4 mins

(Note: For every additional jar used add 1 minute's cooking time.)

6
Store in refrigerator or cool cupboard.

Artificial sweetener can be added if desired.

LEMON AND LIME CORDIAL

INGREDIENTS
Lemons, 3 (large)
Limes, 3
Water, 2–3 cups
Sugar, 1½–2½ cups
Citric acid, 1 teaspoon

METHOD

1
Wash fruit well. Do not peel. Slice roughly and place in a microwave-proof bowl.

2
Add water.

3
Cook on HIGH for 8–10 minutes or until fruit is soft and slightly transparent.

4
Remove from oven and allow to cool.

5
Strain liquid and discard fruit.

6
Reheat liquid on HIGH until boiling.

7
Add sugar and stir until dissolved.

8
Cool and stir in citric acid.

9
Bottle and seal ready for use. For longer keeping, vacuum seal according to instructions on page 32.

10
Store in refrigerator or a cool cupboard.

Orange Cordial

INGREDIENTS
Oranges, 6 (large)
Water, 2–3 cups
Sugar, 1½–2½ cups
Citric acid, 1 teaspoon

METHOD

1
Wash fruit well. Do not peel. Slice roughly and place in a microwave-proof bowl.

2
Add water.

3
Cook on HIGH for 8–10 minutes or until fruit is soft and slightly transparent.

4
Remove from oven and allow to cool.

5
Strain liquid and discard fruit.

6
Reheat liquid on HIGH until boiling.

7
Add sugar and stir until dissolved.

8
Cool and stir in citric acid.

9
Bottle and seal ready for use. For longer keeping, vacuum seal according to instructions on page 32.

10
Store in refrigerator or a cool cupboard.

Orange and Lemon Cordial

INGREDIENTS
Oranges, 4 (large)
Lemons, 2 (large)
Water, 2–3 cups
Sugar, 1½–2½ cups
Citric acid, 1 teaspoon

METHOD

1
Wash fruit well. Do not peel. Slice roughly and place in a microwave-proof bowl.

2
Add water.

3
Cook on HIGH for 8–10 minutes or until fruit is soft and slightly transparent.

4
Remove from oven and allow to cool.

5
Strain liquid and discard fruit.

6
Reheat liquid on HIGH until boiling.

7
Add sugar and stir until dissolved.

8
Cool and stir in citric acid.

9
Bottle and seal ready for use. For longer keeping, vacuum seal according to instructions on page 32.

10
Store in refrigerator or a cool cupboard.

PINEAPPLE CORDIAL

INGREDIENTS
Pineapple, 1 (large)
Water, 2–3 cups
Sugar, 1½–2½ cups
Citric acid, 1 teaspoon

METHOD

1
Remove pineapple top and base. Wash fruit well. Do not peel. Chop roughly and place in a microwave-proof bowl.

2
Add water.

3
Cook on HIGH for 15–20 minutes or until skin is soft and slightly transparent.

4
Remove from oven and allow to cool.

5
Strain liquid and discard fruit.

6
Reheat liquid on HIGH until boiling.

7
Add sugar and stir until dissolved.

8
Cool and stir in citric acid. Yellow food colouring (2–3 drops) may be added if desired.

9
Bottle and seal ready for use. For longer keeping, vacuum seal according to instructions on page 32.

10
Store in refrigerator or a cool cupboard.

8

FRUIT ROLL-UPS

Fruit roll-ups (sometimes called fruit confectionery or fruit leather) can be made quite successfully in your microwave oven from fresh or preserved fruits. They are delicious served with coffee, and children appreciate them in their lunch boxes or just to nibble as a tasty source of energy and nourishment.

Using your microwave to make fruit roll-ups eliminates the long drawn-out process normally involved. Most fruits can be used, but those included here are the most popular.

FRUIT	*INGREDIENTS*
Apples	Fresh or preserved apple puree, 2 cups Sugar, 2 tablespoons Glucose, 2 tablespoons Cinnamon or ground ginger, ½ teaspoon
Apricots	Fresh or preserved apricot puree (drained), 2 cups Sugar, 2 tablespoons Glucose, 2 tablespoons Nutmeg, ground, ½ teaspoon
Peaches	Fresh or preserved peach puree (drained), 2 cups Sugar, 2 tablespoons Glucose, 2 tablespoons
Rhubarb	Fresh or preserved rhubarb puree (drained), 2 cups Sugar, 2 tablespoons Glucose, 2 tablespoons

FRUIT ROLL-UPS

METHOD

1
Prepare puree by peeling fruit, removing any seeds or stones and cutting up roughly.

2
Place in a 1-litre (or larger) casserole or a microwave-proof bowl.

3
Cook uncovered on HIGH for 3–4 minutes or until fruit is tender.

4
Remove from oven and allow to cool.

5
Puree in a blender or Mouli or with a potato masher.

6
Return to bowl with all other ingredients. Add food colouring if desired.

7
Cook on HIGH, still uncovered, until mixture is thick and tacky, approximately 15–18 minutes.

8
Divide mixture into 2 portions. (These will have to be cooked separately, in turn.)

9
Spread one portion directly onto carousel plate until 6 mm (¼ in) thick and about 15 cm (6 in) in diameter.

10
Cook on DEFROST for 12–15 minutes or until rubbery.

11
Remove carousel from oven and allow to cool.
12
Repeat steps 9–11 with second portion
13
Roll up and slice, or cut into shapes. (Children seem to prefer the strips.)
14
Store in plastic wrap or bag or other non-airtight container (otherwise they sweat.)

For preserved fruit, remove from jar, strain off any juices, then follow steps 5–11.

Conversion Table

Abbreviations

g	gram(s)
kg	kilogram(s)
mm	millimetre(s)
cm	centimetre(s)
oz	ounce(s)
lb	pound(s)
in	inch(es)

Measures

6 mm	¼ in
1 cm	½ in
2.5 cm	1 in
3 cm	1 ¼ in
5 cm	2 in
8 cm	3 in
10 cm	4 in
15 cm	6 in
20 cm	8 in
25 cm	10 in
30 cm	12 in

Dry weights

15 g	½ oz
30 g	1 oz
60 g	2 oz
90 g	3 oz
125 g	4 oz
190 g	6 oz
250 g	8 oz
375 g	12 oz
500 g	1 lb
1 kg	2 lbs

Liquid measures

5 ml	1 teaspoon	
10 ml	1 dessertspoon	
20 ml	1 tablespoon	
62 ml	3 tablespoons	¼ cup
83 ml	4 tablespoons	⅓ cup
125 ml	6 tablespoons	½ cup
500 ml	1 pint	2 cups
1 litre	2 pints	4 cups

INDEX

Alternative sweeteners, 7
Apple
    and blackberry jam, 36
    and date chutney, 56
    and ginger chutney, 57
    and raspberry spread, 72
    and rhubarb jam, 36
    butter, 65
    puree, 15
    roll-ups, 85
    sauce, 50
Apples, bottled, 14
Apricot
    and pineapple jam, 37
    butter, 66
    jam, 37
    roll-ups, 85
    sugarless fruit spread, 72
Apricots, bottled, 16

Banana
    and apple sugarless spread, 72
    and mango sugarless spread, 72
Barbecue sauce, 49
Berries, bottled, 17
Berry jam, 38
Bottled fruit
    apples, 14
    apple puree, 15
    apricots, 16
    berries, 17
    cantaloupe, 18
    cherries, 19
    cherry plums, 20
    citrus fruit, 21
    fruit salad, 22
    mangoes, 23
    peaches, 24
    pears, 25
    pineapple, 26
    plums, 27
    tomatoes, 28
    two fruits, 29
Bottling
    see Bottled fruit & 'Just fruit' bottling
Brine, 55

Cantaloupe
    bottled, 18
Cherries, bottled, 19
Cherry jam, 38
Cherry plums
    bottled, 20
Chutneys
    apple and date, 56
    apple and ginger, 57
    red tomato, 60
    rhubarb, 61
Chutneys, relishes and pickles, 53-63
    brine, 55
    spiced vinegar, 54
    spices, 55
    sugar, 55
    vinegar, 54
Citric acid, 9
Citrus fruit
    bottled, 21
Common pitfalls, bottling, 13
Cooking times for bottling, 8, 10
Cooling bottled fruit, 10
Cordials
    lemon and lime, 81
    orange, 82
    orange and lemon, 83
    pineapple, 84
Covering the bowl, 3
Crunchy peanut butter, 67
Cumberland sauce, 43
Curry sauce, 45

Discolouration of
  bottled fruit, 10

Equipment, 4

Fig
  and ginger jam, 39
  jam, 39
Fruit
  juice, 77
  nectar, 80
Fruit and nut butters
  apple, 65
  apricot, 66
  crunchy peanut, 67
  lemon, 68
  orange, 69
  passionfruit, 70
Fruit drinks and cordials, 77-84
Fruit roll-ups
  apples, 85
  apricots, 85
  peaches, 85
  rhubarb, 85
Fruit salad, bottled, 22

Horseradish sauce, 46
Hot choko relish, 58

Jam, making
  method, 35
  pectin, 32-3
  recipes, 36-42
  setting point, 31
  storage, 32
  vacuum sealing, 32
  warming jars, 31
Jams, low-sugar
  apple and apricot, 36
  apple and rhubarb, 36
  apricot, 37
  apricot and pineapple, 37
  berry, 38
  cherry, 38
  fig, 39
  fig and ginger, 39
  mango and pineapple, 40
  melon and ginger, 40
  peach, 41
  pear and ginger, 41
  pineapple, 42
  plum, 42
Jars
  preserving, 4
  recycled, 4
  spacing of, 3
  warming, 31
'Just fruit' bottling
  citric acid, 9
  cooking times, 8, 10
  cooling, 10
  'dos and don'ts', 11
  preparing and packing, 9
  preventing discolouration, 10
  problems and remedies, 13
  sealing, 10
  storing, 11
  sweeteners, 7

Lemon
  and lime cordial, 81
  butter, 68
Low-sugar whole fruit jams
  see Jams, low-sugar

Mango
  and banana sugarless spread, 72
  and pineapple jam, 40
Mangoes, bottled, 23
Melon and ginger jam, 40
Microwave
  bowl, 3
  jars in, 3
  metal in, 3
  power variations, 3
  setting, 3

Orange
  and lemon cordial, 83
  butter, 69
  cordial, 82

Passionfruit butter, 70

Peach
  jam, 41

roll-ups, 85
Peaches, bottled, 24
Peanut butter, crunchy, 67
Pear and ginger jam, 41
Pears, bottled, 25
Pectin, 32-3
Pickled gherkins, 59
Pickles
    gherkins, 59
    zucchini, 63
Pineapple
    and mango jam, 40
    bottled, 26
    cordial, 84
    jam, 42
Pitfalls, bottling, 13
Plum
    chutney spread, 74
    jam, 42
    sauce, 51
Plums, bottled, 27
Preparing and packing fruit for bottling, 9
Preserved fruit
    see Bottled fruit & 'Just fruit' bottling

Red tomato chutney, 60
Red tomato chutney spread, sugarless, 76
Relishes
    hot choko, 58
    sweetcorn, 62
Rhubarb
    chutney, 61
    roll-ups, 85

Savoury sauces, low-sugar
    apple, 50
    barbecue, 49
    Cumberland, 43
    curry, 45
    horseradish, 46
    no-tears, 48
    plum, 51
    tartare, 49
    tomato, 46
    tomato plum, 52
Sealing
    bottled fruit, 10
    jams, 32
Setting point, 31
Spiced vinegar, 54
Spices, 55
Sterilising equipment, 5
Storing
    bottled fruit, 11
    jams, 32
Sugarless fruit spreads
    apple and raspberry, 72
    apricot, 72
    banana and apple, 72
    blackberry, 72
    blackberry and plum, 72
    cherry and cantaloupe, 72
    mango and banana, 72
    plum, 72
    plum and apple, 72
    plum chutney, 74
    red tomato, 76
Sweetcorn relish, 62
Sweeteners for bottling, 7

Tartare sauce, 49
Tomato
    chutney, 60
    juice, 78
    plum sauce, 52
    sauce, 46
    sauce, no tears, 48
Tomatoes, bottled, 28
Two fruits, bottled, 29

Vacuum sealing
    jams, 32
    sauces, 43
Vegetables, health warning, 4
Vinegar, spiced, 54

Whole-fruit low-sugar jams
    see Jams, low-sugar

Zucchini pickles, 63

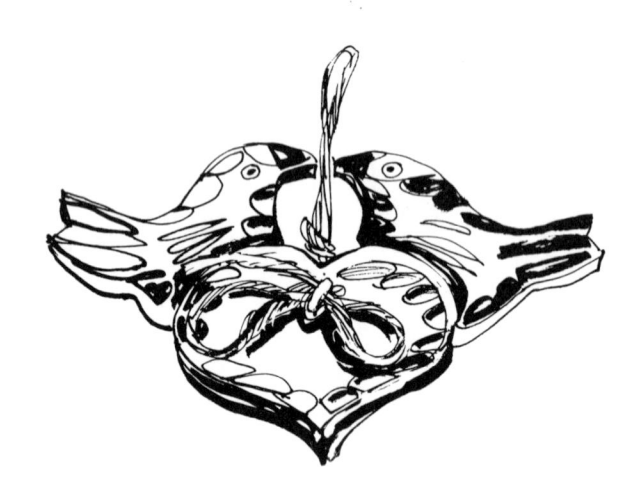